Reader's digest | **Quintessential Guide** to

SAVING
MONEY

Reader's digest | **Quintessential Guide** to

SAVING MONEY

An A to Z of Ingenious Tips for Stretching Your Dollars

The Best Advice, Straight to the Point!

Reader's
digest

The Reader's Digest Association, Inc. New York, NY/Montreal

A READER'S DIGEST BOOK

The Reader's Digest Quintessential Guide to Saving Money contains material first published in *Dollar Savvy, Discounts, Deals, and Steals,* and *13 Things They Won't Tell You.*

All photos and illustrations: © Shutterstock.

Library of Congress Cataloging-in-Publication Data
Reader's digest quintessential guide to saving money / by the editors of Reader's digest.
    pages cm.
    ISBN 978-1-62145-248-5 -- ISBN 978-1-62145-249-2 (Epub) 1. Home economics--Miscellanea.
2. Consumer education--Miscellanea. 3. Waste minimization--Miscellanea. 4. Housekeeping--Cost control--Miscellanea. 5. Saving and investment--Miscellanea. I. Reader's Digest Association. II. Title: Quintessential guide to saving money.
    TX162.2.R43 2016
    640.73--dc23
                                    2015011568

We are committed to both the quality of our products and the service we provide to our customers. We value your comments, so please feel free to contact us.
        The Reader's Digest Association, Inc.
        Adult Trade Publishing
        44 South Broadway
        White Plains, NY 10601

For more Reader's Digest products and information, visit our website:
        www.rd.com (in the United States)
        www.readersdigest.ca (in Canada)

Printed in China

10 9 8 7 6 5 4 3 2 1

Contents

An **A** to **Z** of Extraordinary Savings

Money, money, money. It's the topic of the day, isn't it? No matter how the economy is doing in general, few of us are doing as well as we would like. It's no wonder that America is talking constantly about savings and smart spending!

Boil it down, and you have a choice of two ways to look at the green stuff. The first is the pessimistic approach: Money (or the lack of) is a challenge, a burden, a source of worry and fret. To that approach, we shout an emphatic "Phooey!" The second approach? Well, that's what this book is all about.

The Reader's Digest Quintessential Guide to Saving Money is built on the old-fashioned values and joys of cleverness, frugality, simplicity, and family as the best source of happiness. In this alternative approach, money is never a burden, but instead, a simple tool to be used wisely, as we see fit, to achieve the bigger goals we have for ourselves and our loved ones. The way we see it, America is beginning to wake up from a 30-year buying spree that was neither very helpful for our nation, nor all that healthy for our mental (or physical) health. Today, thanks to some admittedly challenging economic and environmental wake-up calls, we are returning to some old-fashioned American values about what really matters—and what doesn't.

But this does NOT mean we are suddenly a nation of penny-pinchers. This book is all about making smart buying choices everywhere, from how we shop for dinner to the best way to travel, and the most enjoyable ways to live. Reduce waste and excess? Absolutely. Deprive ourselves of the things we love and enjoy? Absolutely not.

And you know what? It's never been a better time to be a consumer! There are more choices now than ever before to buy exactly what you want, often at better prices than ever before (thank you, Internet!). Home-improvement centers have made fixing up your home simple, inexpensive, and amazingly fun. Farmers' markets have made cooking fresh, healthy food easier and cheaper than ever. Entertaining ourselves has never been more of a breeze, thanks to the revolution in home electronics. Live frugally and smartly, and the opportunity for joy and contentment has never been greater. Try any combination of the endlessly savvy tips in this book, and you'll be amazed by the amount of money you've easily and painlessly left in the bank.

This guide does not cover every single way you can save money. We don't talk about maintaining a savings account or building for retirement in the far-off future. Those are important subjects, but we have a different goal. We decided to focus entirely on ingenious advice for everyday life—and lots of it. Use just a fraction of the advice in these pages, and you will save a fortune and create a whole lot of smiles. The attitude behind the book is one we hope you find contagious: Life is good; money is within your control; and with a little bit of good advice, your future is looking so much brighter!

Air conditioner

Don't work alone. Team up your air conditioner with a ceiling fan to spread cool air throughout the room. Using both at the same time lets you raise the air conditioner temperature by five degrees, which in turn lowers your cooling costs.

Stick with the program. Install a programmable thermostat for your air conditioner and cut down on your utility bill. Set it for several degrees warmer at night or when no one is home; you can save up to 10 percent on your cooling costs for every degree above 78 you raise the thermostat.

Don't light up your thermostat. Keep heat-generating appliances like lamps, computers, and televisions away from your air-conditioning thermostat. Their heat will trick the air conditioner into running longer.

Keep it clear. Make sure your air-conditioning vents are not blocked by furniture or other obstructions. (You don't want to pay to cool the back of your couch!)

Seal the leaks. Save on cooling costs by keeping the cool air you've paid for in your house. Seal or caulk dryer vents, pipes entering the house, and electrical outlets as well as drafty windows and doors. You'll keep warm air inside in the winter, too.

Shoot for the sky. Aim the vents of your room air conditioner at the ceiling, and let the cool air float down to you. You'll get more bang for your cooling buck (by cooling the room from top to bottom, rather than in just one spot), plus you'll have better air circulation as the cold air drifts down.

Air freshener

Use a towel, not a spray can. Don't spend money on chemical scents that make you sneeze! You can eliminate odors in your house by soaking a hand towel in white vinegar, wringing it out completely, and swinging it over your head like a lasso a few times. You'll save the cost of air freshener and get a little exercise, too.

Alternative medicines

Make alternate arrangements. Surprisingly enough, alternative medicine—including acupuncture and massage therapy—may be less expensive than traditional treatments for some chronic health problems (depending on your insurance plan). Check your insurance policy for details.

Antacid

Don't be sour. Forget about spending money on antacid at the pharmacy. Next time you have heartburn, acid indigestion, sour stomach, or an upset stomach, simply mix ½ teaspoon of baking soda into ½ cup of water (4 fluid ounces) until the baking soda dissolves completely. Then drink up for more settled times.

Flying high
8 secrets to scoring cheap airfares

Soaring fuel prices, exorbitant ticket-change fees, luggage surcharges, and even fees for seat selection—it seems that travelers just can't catch a break on airfare prices these days. Don't let these "gotchas" get you down: There are still tons of bargains to be had on flights. You can find amazing ticket prices with just a few clicks on your computer or a few phone calls. The next time a beach in Hawaii (or your family reunion) beckons, follow our secrets to getting the best travel deals:

1. **Browse the big travel websites first.** There was a time not so long ago when, if you wanted to book a flight, you would either book directly with the airline or through a travel agent. These days, trip planning through Internet travel sites like Travelocity, Expedia, and Orbitz is more the norm than the exception: You'll not only get a sense about which dates have the best fares to your destination, but you'll also get a ballpark estimate for how much your preferred itinerary will cost you. But wait! Don't book your ticket quite yet . . .

2. **Try mixing and matching airports.** It's sometimes cheaper to take a return flight to a different airport than the one you flew out of. Try this little trick: Say, for example, you want to fly from Newark, New Jersey, to Los Angeles. Just for kicks, search for a return flight to a different airport in the region, such as John F. Kennedy International Airport in New York. (Some airline websites allow you to search this way by clicking a "search nearby airports" button on their reservations pages.) You'd be surprised to find how often ticket prices plummet if you have this kind of flexibility. Of course, this plan doesn't work if you've parked your car at the other airport!

3. **For even deeper discounts, click on your preferred carrier's website.** Now that travel sites like Expedia are doing such brisk business, airlines are fighting for their own pieces of

the profits. Many carriers now offer lowest-price-guaranteed fares on their own websites, and waive the booking fees that the big travel sites often tack on to your reservation. And if you're wondering why you're not finding fares for some of your favorite bargain airlines—like Southwest or JetBlue—on these big travel sites, it's because these airlines don't always release their inventory to travel superstores. That's yet another reason to do some extra sleuthing on your preferred carrier's web page before finalizing your reservations.

4. **Fly in the morning.** Early-morning flights are generally much less expensive than midmorning and afternoon flights because later flights are more convenient for many travelers. Taking an early-morning flight also reduces the likelihood that your plane will be delayed—there's no flight before yours to hold you up! And because there's nothing good to eat on planes anymore, you can catch up on your z's and arrive at your destination refreshed and ready to see the sights.

5. **Pretend that you're flying solo.** Airline search engines mess with your head a little when it comes to booking your family's travel. Consider: If you're booking a flight for you, your spouse, and your cousin Larry, you're going to type "3"

when the site asks you how many tickets you want to buy. The truth is, sometimes you'll get a cheaper rate by booking seats individually, because single seats (especially middle seats in the back of the plane) often go unsold. Airlines jump at the chance to get rid of them. If you're booking over the telephone, ask the reservationist to check the prices of two single seats versus two together.

6. **Make it your "business" to get a first-class ticket for the price of a coach ticket.** Airlines don't exactly advertise this fact, but it's possible to book a business-

or first-class ticket for the same price as a regular (not discounted) coach fare. They're called Q-up, Y-up, or Z-up fares, and they all amount to first-class upgrades of coach fares, according to Laura Powell, a longtime travel journalist and expert. Airlines created the fares to benefit business travelers, many of whom work for companies that don't allow them to buy first-class tickets. The website farecompare. com helps you search for those deals.

7. **Redeem frequent-flyer miles wa-a-a-a-y in advance.** Here's a fact that airlines won't be advertising anytime soon: They release their booking schedules a whopping 330 days in advance, according to Anne Banas, executive editor of SmarterTravel.com. If you want to use your frequent-flyer miles during a peak travel time—say, Christmas— you should start dialing those airlines up around Valentine's Day.

8. Know that procrastination sometimes pays off.

Generally speaking, prices on airfares are relatively constant until about 21 days before a flight is set to take off. At this point, prices start to climb. But occasionally prices drop, if only for a short while, 72 to 48 hours before your flight takes off. Why? The industry term is "distressed inventory," which translates as "empty airline seats" to you and me. If you have nothing to do this weekend, it's worth calling a few carriers or checking their websites (some even send e-mail alerts about last-minute bargains). You may score that $400 flight to Miami for $200 or less!

Should I book my flight on Priceline.com?

Nowadays Priceline.com offers standard packages without bidding, like the other major travel sites, and is worth checking out for their own unique deals. But their fame, of course, came from users bidding for services offered. Though some folks might be intimidated by the "name your own price" gimmick, Priceline is a great way to save some dough on flights that originate in the United States. That said, keep in mind when booking airline tickets that Priceline can place you on any flight (3 a.m. does count) during the 24-hour period of your departure date.

Appliances

The price will floor you. Ask your appliance retailer if you can buy the floor model of the appliance you want for a reduced price.

Don't be a fan. Shop for major purchases like appliances during sporting events like the Super Bowl or the World Series. Stores will be empty, and the salespeople will be ready and willing to negotiate so they can rack up some sales. You may easily knock at least 2 percent off the original purchase price of whatever you want to buy.

Art

Book it. Frame pictures from art books or magazines (that you own, of course) to spruce up your walls. Look for nice, inexpensive frames to highlight your masterpieces.

ATMs

Take only what you need. On average, consumers withdraw $60 per week from an ATMs. And most consumers have no idea where that money goes. Figure out how much cash you really need each week, and take only that amount out of the ATM. You won't overspend because you won't have extra money in your wallet.

Be faithful— to your bank.

Take money out of only your bank's ATM. You can be charged up to $3 by your bank for taking money out of another bank's machine, and then be charged again by the other bank. Don't pay another bank for access to your money.

B

Baths

Just say no. Compare the amount of water you use in the shower to the amount you use in a bath. Next time you shower, plug the bathtub and see how much water fills the tub. If there's less water than in your normal bath, you'll save money by taking a shower. Remember: an average bath uses 30 to 50 gallons of water, while a four-minute shower with a low-flow shower head uses only 10 gallons. Take short showers and save.

Battery

Baking soda for your car battery. Your car battery needs to be clean to keep working. You can remove corrosion and keep the battery clean with a mixture of 1 tablespoon baking soda and 1 cup of water. Use the solution to wash the outside of the battery (being careful not to let it get into the battery). Rinse it off with clean water and wipe to dry.

Belts

Cut it down to size. Don't toss a belt that no longer fits or doesn't work with your clothes. Size it to fit your pet as a collar.

Birdbath

Give the birds a bath (without taking one). Ignore fancy and expensive birdbaths at your garden or birding store. Fashion an equally useful bird-bath from an old pan on top of a flowerpot. Fill it with water and watch the birds flock to it.

Blinds

Be neutral. Buy blinds in a neutral color. You'll still be able to use them later if you change the color scheme of the room you're decorating now.

Books

Round up reading material. There's no need to buy books when you want to read something new. Organize an ongoing book swap with your church or a social or community group. Everyone brings in their latest and greatest reads and swaps them for others. Keep the books on an accessible shelf; you may need several shelves if your collection is a success!

Boots and shoes

Protect your sole. Make your boots and all your shoes last 10 times longer by going from the shoe store to the shoe repair and having sole protectors or heel and toe taps put on your new footwear. The protectors cost less than $20 and potentially save you hundreds since it's usually the soles that wear out first.

Let your footwear breathe. Don't store any shoes or boots in the attic or the basement during the off-season. The shifts in temperature will prematurely age them. Place them in a closet that allows air to circulate, and they'll last longer, saving you money and (yet another) a trip to the store.

Bottles as boot trees. Prolong the life of your boots by storing them with unusual boot trees. Put a clean, empty 1-liter soda bottle in each boot to help it retain its shape. You won't have to pay for boot trees—or new boots.

Buttons

Old buttons, new look. Keep nice, fancy, or unusual buttons when you recycle or toss worn-out clothing. You can use them to change the look of a garment that's starting to bore you or to enliven a plain shirt that needs a little pizzazz.

Calendar

Save $15 by getting a calendar for free. Where? Try banks, insurance agencies, card stores, and your mail—you may find calendars from charities you support as well as from businesses you've used.

Candles

Keep your candles cold. Store your candles in the freezer for a longer burn life.

Car

Don't waste by waiting. If you plan to wait for someone in your idling car for more than one minute, turn the car off to save gas. You'll use less fuel starting up the car than leaving it on for even this short a time.

Warm your heart, not your car. Today's cars do not need to be warmed up for more than 30 seconds. You car will warm up as you drive. If you warm it up in the driveway, you're just wasting gas.

Car wash

Fill up and wash up. Some gas stations offer free or cut-rate car washes when you stop to get gas.

Carpet

Go to pieces. Next time you need to replace your carpet, think about using carpet tiles for busy areas such as hallways and entryways. If a piece of the carpet gets stained or worn, you can simply replace the tile, rather than the whole carpet.

Pay more to pay less. Invest in a good-quality pad for under your carpet. It will protect the carpet from wear and tear, and let you buy a less expensive carpet.

Carpet cleaner

Salt it away. Don't use an expensive carpet cleaner next time you experience a nasty red wine spill on your carpet. Save that $5 to $10 and simply pour a pile of good old table salt on the spill. Leave the salt on until it dries, and then vacuum it up. The stain is gone!

Share it and save. Rent a carpet-cleaning machine for you and a neighbor, and split the cost. You can save big on a one-day rental.

Sprinkle on seltzer. As soon as food hits your rug, wipe up the excess and then sprinkle it liberally with seltzer or club soda. Scrub with a brush, sprinkling on more seltzer or soda as needed. Blot dry with a towel.

Cash

Stash the cash. Cutting impulse spending can save big bucks, so if this is your personal bugaboo, try keeping only $20 to $40 in your wallet. The less you have in cash, the less you're likely to spend on impulse purchases. That $4 latte at the coffee shop will look a lot less appealing if it leaves you with only $16 for the rest of the day!

Cash register

Watch it like a hawk. Cash registers, as well as humans, make errors, so watch the register carefully to make sure it rings up the right price for the right item. You might get overcharged if the register mistakes your cream cheese for Brie or if it hasn't been programmed with the current sale prices. Many grocery stores will give the item for free or at a sharp discount if the register (whether operated by a cashier or you on a self-checkout line) charges you the wrong amount.

Cat

It's the cat's meow. Save on vet bills by adding 1/8 to 1/4 teaspoon of olive oil to your cat's food. It will help prevent hairballs and keep your cat's digestive system purring along.

Cell phone

Talk isn't cheap. The average cell phone user faces a $60 bill each month, including taxes and miscellaneous fees. If you talk less than 200 minutes a month, you may be better off using a pay-as-you-go plan (as long as it charges 25 cents a minute or less). You can easily save $45 a month with a prepaid plan.

Extend your battery life. Try to run your battery out before recharging, at least every other time, for the longest battery life. Avoid buying a new cell phone battery and give your electric bill a break in the process by shutting your cell phone off before you go to sleep. Just remember to turn it back on in the morning!

Checks

Check it off your list. Is your bank charging a lot for printing your checks? If so, check out independent printers: most of them charge about half what your bank does for the same service. Try Checks Unlimited (800-210-0468 or checksunlimited.com) or Checks in the Mail (800-733-4443 or checksinthemail.com), or do an Internet search for "personal check printers," which will turn you up an additional range of printers such as checkswithstyle.com or checkworks.com. If you've ever wanted checks with John Deere tractors on them, an independent printer is the way to go!

Chicken

Buy it whole. Never buy chicken parts when you can buy the whole thing and make more meals from it, for pennies on the pound. Forget about fancy butchering: using strong kitchen shears, cut the chicken up the breast bone, up the back bone, and then cut those halves in half again. Cut off wings and legs, and you now have the kind of pieces that you'd pay hefty bucks for. Never again!

Coffee

Treat yourself—to a gift card. Buying a premium coffee regularly is the bugaboo of personal finance advisers, who see it as the ultimate waste of money, but it is okay to get one now and then. (Let's face it, they can be pretty tasty!) If you're inclined to overdo, buy a gift card for yourself for a budgeted amount each month, and enjoy every frothy, flavored cupful until the card runs out.

Cut the cost of home-brewed gourmet coffee. Even coffee made at home can be expensive, if you have expensive coffee tastes in fancy beans and roast. But you can mix the pleasure with savings if you combine one part of your favorite gourmet coffee with one part of a much less expensive store brand, and enjoy your high-end coffee tastes at a fraction of the cost.

Nothing's better than a leisurely morning and a bottomless cup of coffee, but warming the coffee pot all morning isn't good for your electric bill—or your coffee, which will take on a flat, bitter flavor as all the essential oils evaporate. Brew directly into a thermal pot or pour your fresh-brewed coffee into a thermos, then turn off the coffeemaker, and treasure your savings.

Pretend it's a day at the office. Even if you're drinking your coffee at home, think about buying it at an office-supply superstore, such as Staples or Office Depot. You may find substantial savings on hot chocolate, tea, coffee, creamer, and sugar at the same place you get a good deal on your pencils and printer ink.

Coins

Hoard loose change. Dump your loose change into a jar at the end of every day, and once every six months or so (or while you can still lift the jar!), bring your change to a local bank that has a coin-counting machine. It's important to take them to a bank, which likely won't charge you a fee for the counting, rather than to one of the commercial coin-counting machines you see in grocery stores, which will deduct 10 percent of your hard-earned change. Ka-ching!

Computer

Think small to save big. Buy a laptop computer: it uses less energy than an Energy Star–rated desktop computer and monitor. A typical laptop draws from 15 to 25 watts when being used, while a conventional PC and monitor draw 150 watts. You'll be pleased with the evidence on your utility bill.

Go to sleep. Your computer continues to use energy even when you're not using it. In fact, you can cut its power demand by up to 90 percent if you make it automatically "sleep" after 20 or 30 minutes of non-use. (See your manual for programming instructions—it's usually a simple adjustment.) And when you finish a session of Internet surfing or e-mailing, turn it off altogether.

Confetti

Celebrate the savings. There's nothing more festive than a handful of confetti at a party, but don't spend money buying little bits of paper. Save leftover wrapping paper—even small pieces will work—and use a hole punch or little scissors to create lots of circles or squares for colorful confetti. Use your homegrown confetti to celebrate family birthdays, News Year's Eve, or any happy occasion. (You can even vacuum it up into a clean hand vac to use again!)

Consignment shopping

Pick your target carefully. One obvious way to cut back on clothing costs is to check out consignments shops. But don't choose just any consignment shop: find one close to a wealthy neighborhood, where you may be surprised to find stacks of hardly or never-worn clothes, many from top designers and some items with the tags still on. You'll get amazing bargains on extraordinary clothes you won't find elsewhere.

Contact lenses

See your way through the mail. Save up to 50 percent on contact lenses and more on the necessary accessories (fluid and cleaning apparatus) by ordering through the mail. You can order the exact type of lenses you currently wear—not a lesser brand—at a substantial discount by phone at 1-800-Contacts or online at 1800contacts.com.

Container gardening

Skimp on the soil. Save money on potting soil by using only as much as your plant needs—not what the deep container dictates. Put broken-up polystyrene chunks or packing "peanuts" at the bottom of the pot (making sure to keep the drainage hole clear), then add enough potting soil for your plant. You'll benefit from a lighter pot as well as a heavier wallet, and you'll find your pot drains better when it's not heavily packed with soil down to the bottom.

Cottage cheese

Turn it on its head. Store your container of cottage cheese upside down in the refrigerator. It will last twice as long than when stored right side up.

Credit card

Edit your credit. Lose the temptation to spend by locking away your credit cards. Don't cancel them (it can hurt your credit score); instead, put them in a safe place, keeping only one in your wallet.

Dentist

Find a tooth trainee. If there's a local dental school near you, you may be able to get free or almost-free dental checkups and work done by supervised students (assuming your teeth are in good condition). Call to ask about the school's policy and go in for a cleaning to assess the school and see if you're comfortable. Chances are you can get excellent care for a fraction of the usual price.

Have a plan. Consider getting a dental plan rather than dental insurance. You pay an annual fee, ranging from $100 to $150, and get a 20 to 60 percent discount from participating dentists. Visit discount-dental.net or dentalplans.com to get more information and sign up.

Dentures

Do it yourself. Don't spend money over and over on expensive denture-cleaning products. You can clean dentures easily and inexpensively at home with a soft toothbrush and a teaspoon of baking soda. Scrub gently and rinse in clear water. Then place the dentures in a small, microwave-safe container just big enough to hold them (a coffee mug, for example) and cover them with water. Add a tablespoon of white vinegar and microwave on high for two minutes. Allow to cool in the solution overnight, then in the morning rinse and wear. You can only do this if your dentures have no metal parts, but the microwave will kill bacteria far more effectively than anything you can buy.

Deodorant

Smell the savings. Save a fast few bucks by dusting baking soda under your arms instead of using commercial deodorant.

Detangler

Tame your hair for the price of conditioning it. Make your conditioner work overtime as a detangler. Simply mix 1 part conditioner with 5 parts water and spray the mixture on your wet hair, then comb. You'll be impressed by the versatility of your conditioner!

Save $60 with a magnifying glass.

If you're the typical telephone user, you dial 411 twice a month—and at up to $2.50 a call, you're losing out on $60 a year. Save all that money by looking up the number you need in a phone book, using a magnifying glass to help read the small type, if necessary. Or try Whitepages.com, Superpages.com, or Switchboard.com to find phone numbers for free online.

Directory assistance

411 for free. If you don't mind listening to a few ads, dial 800-373-3411 for free directory assistance. You'll save up to $2.50 per call.

Discount store

Give it a hug. Discount stores tempt you not only with their excellent bargains, but also with their "I don't know what I was thinking when I bought this" impulse buys. How can you avoid these temptations? Avoid the shopping cart. Buy only what you can carry in your arms. You'll end up buying only what you really need and want.

Dishwasher

Give your dishwasher the vinegar treatment. Every six months, pour a cup of distilled white vinegar in the unit, and run the regular wash cycle. The vinegar will dissolve soap residue and minerals that have collected throughout the dishwasher.

Fix chipped racks pronto. If the plastic coating on your dishwasher racks is chipped, the damage will spread as water works its way under the coating and causes the rack to rust. As soon as you notice a chip, go to your hardware store or home center and pick up a can of ReRACK, a synthetic rubber coating. Just brush the stuff on the damaged area following the instructions.

Give the bottom a once-over. Get in the habit of taking a quick look at the bottom of your dishwasher after each usage for items that might have fallen through the racks or gotten stuck in the drain. A loose fork can do a lot of damage, as can an errant piece of plastic wrap clogging the drain.

Keep the wheels turning. Dishwasher rack jammed? The rollers may be sticking. Turn them by hand to loosen them. If they are worn and no longer round, replace them. Some can be removed by taking out screws; most simply pull off. If a rack sticks because it is bent, replace it. You can get replacement rollers and racks from appliance dealers who carry your machine's brand.

Disposal

Vinegar ice is nice for your disposal. Now and then, feed your garbage disposal a few frozen cubes of white vinegar and then flush with cold water after grinding. You'll help keep the disposal free of clogs and slow drains—and expensive repairs. The vinegar will also keep odors at bay.

Doctor

No longer the doctor's "office." You don't have to go to the doctor's office to get good medical help these days. Try going to CVS, Target, and Walmart, many of which have opened in-store clinics, often run by nurse-practitioners. You don't need an appointment, and you'll get a diagnosis for about $25 to $60 (plus a prescription if you need one)—far less than a typical doctor's office visit.

Dollar bills

Go the paper route. Stop spending coins; they make you think you're not spending much. Instead, use only paper currency to buy everything, and put the change from all your daily purchases into a change bucket (see "Coins" on page 24). You'll be likely to spend less and can save at least $20 a month with this trick.

Dry cleaning

Don't get taken to the cleaners. In fact, you can make out well with dry cleaners if you know when to go. Take in your drapes and bed linens in January, July, or August, when business is slow. Your local cleaner may offer a discount of around 15 percent on large items; since drapes and bed linens can cost several hundred dollars to clean, you'll come out smelling like a rose.

Dryer

Keep it clean. A dirty lint filter forces your dryer to use 30 percent more energy to dry clothes. Clean the lint filter after every load and save a bundle.

Keep it light. Dry lightweight fabrics with lightweight fabrics; save heavier fabrics for another load. The lightweight fabrics will dry faster when they're alone, so they'll spend less time in the dryer. You'll save time, energy, and money.

Not the time for the timer. Stop using the timer when you dry your clothes. You can cut down on energy use by about 15 percent by using the moisture sensor instead. Besides, drying already-dry clothes—which happens when you use the timer—can stress your clothes and reduce their lifespan.

Let it all hang out. Try to use your dryer as infrequently as possible. Instead, hang your clothes on a clothes rack or clothesline to dry. Grandmother's ways were best! You'll save money on electricity, and your clothes (particularly those that contain elastic) will last longer, too.

Dryer sheets

Cut your softener in half. Half a dyer sheet works just as well as a whole one, so cut the sheet in half, and soften two loads for the price of one.

Don't just soften: clean! Put your used dryer sheets to work: dust your TV and computer screens, clean Venetian blinds, polish your bathroom taps, and wipe dry tile surfaces. You can even put them in shoes, wastebaskets, and laundry hampers for a fresh smell. You'll save money on all kinds of cleaning supplies.

How to get the most out of a doctor's appointment

You had to wait weeks for an appointment. Then you sat in the waiting room for 40 minutes. Then you sat 20 minutes more in the examination room. Suddenly, the doctor shows up . . . and in no time, is gone. What should you discuss with your physician, and what should you just leave to the nurse? Here's how to maximize the precious few minutes that you are allotted with your doctor.

STUFF TO SETTLE BEFORE YOU SEE THE DOCTOR

✔ **Insurance issues**
Confirm whether your doctor accepts your health insurance, and always bring your insurance card with you to your appointments (this is especially important when you're seeing a new doctor). That way, you'll know immediately how much your co-pay will be. Doctors don't usually know the nuts and bolts of each carrier's coverage—but the office manager does.

✔ **Records and referrals**
If you're seeing a doctor or specialist for the first time, you want to be sure that he has all of the information that he needs to treat you: Have all of your medical records (including x-rays, MRIs, and hospital surgical records, if applicable) forwarded to the doctor's office before your appointment so that he can study them prior to your meeting. You don't want him to spend his few minutes with you with his nose in a folder. Finally, be sure to bring your referral forms with you, too.

STUFF FOR THE NURSE TO HANDLE

✔ **Vitals and weight**
When your nurse calls you into the exam room, make sure she takes care of these things before your doctor comes in. You've gotten on a scale, urinated in a cup, and had your blood pressure checked so

many times that you could practically log the results in on your own. There's no need to waste time with your doctor on this!

✔ **Knowing whether you're due for yearly tests or shots**

Need a flu shot or a tetanus booster? Think you might be due for a routine colonoscopy? Ask the nurse. She'll consult your records and alert your doctor that these "maintenance" issues need to be taken care of. She might even be able to give you the shots herself.

THE DOCTOR WILL SEE YOU NOW!

✔ **Symptoms and questions**
Most patients wait for the doctors to ask questions. Don't! Quickly let it be known you have several things you want to talk about. Start with all your recent symptoms. However minor these issues may seem to you, be sure to mention that you get headaches every evening after dinner, and point out that suspicious mole.

You may not know whether your symptoms are related to a drug interaction or a virus that's going around, but your doctor will. Now's also the time to ask about how your own well-being might relate to health-care issues you've heard about on the news ("Should I stop taking the cholesterol drug that's been shown to increase the risk of stroke?" "Could my upset stomach be caused by that salmonella outbreak?"). Be sure to write down every ache, pain, and question before you see him: You don't want to forget something important and have to wait for another appointment.

✔ **Self-remedies**
If you have any chronic health issues, tell your doctor what you are doing to treat yourself. For

example, if you have arthritis, you might be doing warm-water aerobics or taking specific vitamin supplements. Find out if what you're doing is safe and effective given your situation.

✔ Test results specifics

Are your blood results in? What were the results of that biopsy? Get your doc to spill the specifics—that means more than just a "pass/fail" answer. Your cholesterol may read "normal" now, but unless you press for the actual numbers, you may not know that you're just two points out of the time-to-worry range. Be sure to bring a notebook and record the actual figures, too.

✔ Everything you're taking, spraying, or rubbing on

Before you see the doc, throw all of those pill bottles on your nightstand into a resealable bag—and don't forget those vitamins, calcium supplements, eyedrops, and skin creams in your medicine cabinet. (A list will suffice if you carefully record the dosage, frequency, and brand that you're taking.) Think about it: How would your doctor

know if another doc prescribed a medication unless you tell her?

Patients "don't think that things like low-dose aspirin or hydrocortisone cream 'count,' because they're nonprescription items," says Mary Nolan, RN, admissions nurse at Baystate Franklin Medical Center in Greenfield, Massachusetts. But knowing about them can make a huge difference in how you're treated: Nolan knows of a patient who was taking atropine eyedrops, which were causing his heart rate to slow down. Until the patient mentioned the drops, the doctor thought he might need a pacemaker!

✔ Changes to your prescription regimen

Once your doctor has taken a look at what you're taking and heard about new symptoms you may be feeling, she may want to tweak

your prescription medication regimen. Here are some questions to ask before she starts scribbling new scripts:

- **Are any of my medications now available in generic form?** Are there any generic alternatives? Medicines come off patent all the time, which means they become generic. Generic, as we all know, is code for "a heck of a lot cheaper" than brand-name prescriptions.

- **How much of that do I really need?** To treat acute symptoms, ask your physician to write a prescription only for the minimum amount of medication that he thinks you'll need. If your condition persists, you can always phone the office and ask for a refill. On the other hand, if you take a drug to treat a chronic condition such as diabetes or arthritis, it may be less expensive to buy three months' worth via mail order rather than a one-month supply.

- **Do you have a sample of that?** Doctors get free samples of the newest and most popular drugs—why shouldn't you get a week or two of free meds? This is an especially good idea if the drug is new to you; if you buy a month's supply and you have a bad reaction to it, you'll be out some serious cash.

- **How much will that new prescription cost me?** Your doctor probably has no idea how much you pay for medications, or how much your prescription plan covers. Speak up about price as soon as she whips out that prescription pad; it's best not to go into sticker shock at the pharmacy!

NEXT STEPS

Don't let the doctor leave without your having complete clarity about what you should be doing as a result of the visit. Should you schedule a return visit? Change vitamins? Do something different for that symptom? Keep a food or sleep log? Do some research? So often, we leave the doctor's office more confused than comforted, in large part because of the speed of it all. So your last conversation with the doctor before she scoots out the door should be a summation that makes clear all your next steps.

DVDs

Check it out. Most large libraries now have a DVD section that offers an excellent selection of up-to-date and classic movies that can be checked out on your regular library card (although you may not find the very latest releases). The rules vary depending on your branch, but generally you can check out as many DVDs as you want for one week, with steep-for-a-library fines, such as $1 per day, beginning on the eighth day. So get those DVDs returned on time and take out a fresh batch!

Education

Study with the experts. The iTunes U app offers dozens of free courses on many academic subjects. Book groups are also a good way to learn about many topics, and the book groups at Goodreads offer you an opportunity to learn from authors and experts—for free! Here you'll find a librarians book club, a mystery book club, a book club devoted to young adult literature, and more. See what interests you at goodreads.com/group.

Electrician

Save on service calls. Unless you have an electrical emergency, don't call the electrician every time you need something fixed. Since you pay a set (and often high) price for each service call, you'll save by having several tasks done at once.

Electronics

Keep the vampires at bay. Electronics and appliances that sport clocks or work by a remote use electricity, even

Energy Star ratings

If you change just one light bulb in your home to an Energy Star–approved bulb, it's as good for the environment as not driving your car for two weeks—and not only is the energy savings good for the planet, but it also adds up to dollars in your pocket. You can make significant changes in your carbon footprint and in your power bill by using products approved by Energy Star, a joint program between the U.S. Environmental Protection Agency and the U.S. Department of Energy. Using Energy Star techniques, advice, strategies, and approved appliances and light bulbs, Americans saved $30 billion on their utility bills in 2013. Make sure you get your share of the savings! Check out the Energy Star website at energystar.gov for a wealth of hugely practical energy-saving techniques.

continued on page 40

13 no-cost ways to reduce energy bills

Small, inexpensive changes to the way you use energy around the house can significantly reduce your energy costs—from heat to hot water. Once you make these changes, the only thing you'll notice are lower bills.

1. **The big chill.** Our experts say that you can save up to $63 per year by washing all your clothes in cold water instead of warm or hot.

2. **Fully loaded.** Full loads of laundry and dishes result in maximum efficiency and help you avoid water waste. Air-dry dishes—and clothes, if you can—for even more savings.

3. **Lose the lint.** If you must dry clothes in a dryer, always clean the lint filter after every load to maintain peak drying efficiency (not to mention reducing the risk of fire).

4. **Separate heavy from light.** Dry towels, bedspreads, and other heavy items separately from lighter-weight items to increase drying efficiency.

5. **You're all wet.** Take showers instead of baths and install a low-flow showerhead to save on water and heat.

6. **No drips allowed.** Fix leaky faucets. Even a little drip can add up to a big-time water bill.

7. **Bundle up.** Insulate your hot water pipes and water heater with approved insulation materials for efficiency. Your heating bills will be reduced up to 10 percent.

8. **Turn it off.** Turn off lights, TVs, computers, and other electronics when they are not in use.

9. **Let there be (better) light.** Replace your most-used conventional incandescent bulbs with long-lasting,

energy-saving compact fluorescent bulbs. Use the sun as your main source of light during the day whenever possible—so open up those drapes and pull up the blinds!

10. Filter savings. Clean or replace air-conditioning and heating-system filters monthly for maximum efficiency.

11. Air-dry for freshness and savings. One of the cleanest, freshest, most frugal ways to dry your clothes is—you guessed it—outside on a line (weather permitting).

12. Do the glow test. Wait until after dark to walk around your house (with a flashlight!) to see what is "glowing." The results will amaze you: your power strips, your computers, your DVD player, your cable box, your microwave oven. Although you may not be actively using them, all of these items in your home are perpetually "on" and eating electricity, unless you pull the plugs when they're not in use.

13. Keep your freezer full. If your freezer is empty, you can be sure that it's working overtime to keep the space icy cold. Remedy this by filling it with a large stone, a bucket, a milk jug filled with water— anything that will take up space; the freezer won't work as hard and therefore will use less electricity.

continued from page 37

when you're not using them. Chargers do, too. In fact, 40 percent of the energy used to run home electronics is devoured when these energy vampires aren't turned off! So literally pull the plug and pull down your energy costs.

'Tis the season to scoop up returns . . . and savings. Shop the clearance section of electronics stores after the holidays. It's a good time to find open-box merchandise or other returned items that can't be sold for full price. You may just find a very merry bargain!

Do some due diligence. A little research can pay you back in spades when it comes to buying new electronics. Whether you're ready for a new TV or you want to buy the grandkids the cutting-edge toy of the moment, go to google.com/shopping. Type in the name of the item you want in the resulting search box, and Google will instantly pull up a list of all the prices for that item that can be found on the Internet, making comparison shopping a breeze!

Entertainment

The more the merrier. Find friends, colleagues, neighbors, and relatives who like the kinds of entertainment you like, and attend concerts, sporting events, and exhibitions for less. Just buy your tickets in bulk, and you'll score a 10 percent (or higher) discount.

Look up savings at the library. You know you can borrow books, CDs, DVDs, magazines, and even more at your library for free, but the library is also the place to find free or discounted passes to local zoos, museums, aquariums, and gardens. Stop by to see how entertaining your library can be.

Save in different seasons. Check out free concerts sponsored by your local community during the summer. During the holidays, look for free concerts at churches and colleges.

Usher in the arts.

Save up to $300 on season tickets to the symphony, opera, ballet, or theater by working as an usher at your local performance hall. Simply call the hall and ask if you can usher, or search the Internet with the words "volunteer," "usher," and the name of your town.

Practice, practice, practice. Many orchestras and other performing arts groups open their rehearsals to the public, free of charge. Find out what's available in your community, and pocket the cost of the performance.

Try out the tunes. Why spend money on an album when you don't know which tracks you'll like? Instead, tune in to Pandora.com and listen to hours of music you know you'll enjoy for free. Simply enter the name of the singer or the song you like, and Pandora will provide you with similar songs. You'll hear music you want, and the price is right.

Eyeglasses

Nail polish for your eyes. Next time you tighten the screw on your glasses (to avoid even bigger trouble), add a spot of clear nail polish across the top of the screw. Your fix will last longer—and your glasses will, too.

Buy two, pay less. Ask for a discount from your eyeglass provider if you plan to buy two pairs of frames at a time.

Think inside the (big) box. Check out warehouse clubs when you're checking out glasses. You'll be amazed by the selection, quality, and—above all—prices. You can easily find a complete pair of glasses (frames and lenses) for under $150, about half what it would cost elsewhere.

Fans

Use fans to keep you warm. Ceiling fans are energy-efficient lifesavers in the summer, but did you know that they're equally helpful in the winter? Use the reverse setting on your fan to push the warm air at ceiling level back down to you.

Let it rest. Your bathroom fan may be doing more harm than good in the winter, if you let it run too long. According to the Department of Energy, a bathroom fan can suck all the nicely warmed air out of your house in just one hour. So give your fan and your furnace and your wallet a break.

Farmers' markets

Shop often—and late. Farmers' markets have the freshest produce and good deals—but you can get even better deals if you shop late in the day. Sellers don't want to bring unsold produce back home, so they often sell their inventory at reduced prices before the market closes. You may find sweet savings of up to 80 percent.

Flowers

Send flowers long-distance, but save by going local. Bypass excessive shipping and processing charges from national floral services and order flowers from a florist in the recipient's town. Find the names and phone numbers of local florists by visiting locateaflowershop.com.

continued on page 48

Free stuff worth getting

Most freebies are barely worth their price—but not these terrific giveaways.

For bargain-hunters, there's only one thing that's more thrilling than getting a good deal: getting something for free! With that in mind, we searched for free items that are actually worth pursuing. Our list barely scratches the surface. Note that many require Internet access, so if you don't have a computer at home, go to your public library and use theirs—that, too, is free! One note: Free offers and website names change fast. While these offers were all available at press time, some may have expired or changed. Our key message: With a little searching, you'll be surprised at all the free stuff you can find!

CARDS, BOOKS, AND OTHER PAPER GOODS

✔ Bibles

We know, Gideon Bibles have been available in hotel rooms almost since the book was written (and yes, they don't mind if you take them, though you might wish to mention it to the hotel). But there are other ways to get a Bible that's new or only slightly used. The easiest way, of course, is to ask a local church; they often have a surplus of copies. Another source is the website biblesforamerica.org. Fill out a request, and they will send you a modern "recovery" version of the Bible. Also, the Church of Jesus Christ of Latter-Day Saints (the Mormons) will send you one for the asking. If you live in the United States or Canada, you can get the King James Version by filling out a form at their website (mormon.org/free-bible) or by calling 877-537-0005 (U.S. only). You'll be asked if Mormon representatives may visit you, and you're free to accept or decline.

Finally, some websites, like bibledatabase.com, offer free digital Bibles and workbooks.

✔ Greeting Cards

With prices climbing to $3, $4, and beyond, the costs of greeting cards are getting out of hand. You can save big money by printing free cards and similar products (like business cards, calendars, gift tags, and more) at printfree.com. All it will cost you is the price of paper and the ink in your printer's cartridge. However, if your well wishes need to arrive at their destination today, send an electronic or e-card from hallmarkecards.com. Cards are sent to the recipient's e-mail address—you can schedule delivery for today, tomorrow, or a few months from now.

✔ Books

If you and your family are all bookworms, your reading habits may be costing you dearly. Your first recourse, obviously, is the public library. But what if they don't have the book you want, or you're stuck waiting weeks for it? Here's how to recycle books and save a few trees in the process: At paperbackswap.com, you list nine books you no longer want and get three credits to order any three books from a member database of nearly six million titles. If someone wants one of the books on your list, you mail it out to them at media rate (usually under $2 per paperback).

✔ Snapshots

These days, almost everyone has a digital camera or a smartphone with a great camera built right into it. Sharing photos with friends and family has never been easier, thanks to photo-sharing and printing websites like shutterfly.com, flickr.com, and snapfish.com. Though these sites' promotions vary from week to week, signing up for a free account with any of them might score you anywhere from 20 to 50 photo prints—sometimes even a poster-size print. You may have to pay a few dollars for shipping, but it's still a great deal.

HEALTH AND BEAUTY

✔ Nutrition Information

Whether you're dieting to lose weight or due to a specific health concern—or if you just want to eat more healthfully—nutritiondata. self.com should be your first stop on the Internet. You can find a complete nutritional analysis for just about every food item (even brand-name products) by entering it into the site's search field. The site's information comes in quite handy, for example, if you're diabetic and want to know how many carbs are hiding in your favorite brand of yogurt.

✔ Health and Beauty Product Samples

Walmart's website (walmart. com) posts lots of free samples and special offers of shampoo, aftershave, skin-care items, and similar products. To locate them, search from the site for "Free Samples." When you see a sample that strikes your fancy, click the highlighted link. In some cases, Walmart will send the item to you; in others, you print out a coupon that you use in the store.

✔ Hearing Aids

If you're hard of hearing or have a child who is, you should know about these charities, which provide hearing aids free of charge:

• **Hear Now** (sotheworldmayhear. org/hearnow, or 800-328-8602), a national nonprofit program for adults, collects and recycles used hearing aids from donors and redistributes them to those in need.

• **The Miracle Ear Children's Foundation** (miracle-ear. com/childrenrequest.aspx or 800-234-5422) provides free hearing aids and services to children 18 years and under from low-income families.

- **The Hearing Impaired Kids Endowment Fund** (thehikefund.org), a philanthropic project of Job's Daughters International, provides about 100 young people under 20 years old with hearing aids every year.

EDUCATION

✔ Online Classes

Prepare to be amazed—and, more important, smarter: free-ed.net offers online courses and tutorials in 120-plus vocational and academic disciplines, all free of charge. Students who never finished high school can prepare for an equivalency diploma, which is earned by taking the General Educational Development (GED) exam. Those interested in, say, the building trades can choose courses in masonry, electrical construction, professional carpentry, and more. If all the free info isn't enough, free-ed.net also has links to a collection of free online textbooks for each course.

✔ SAT Test Preparation

Scoring well on the SAT (formerly called the Scholastic Aptitude Test) college entrance exams can give young people an extra edge when applying to universities. But tutors and test-prep courses are expensive—as much as $900 for six weeks of practice sessions. You can prepare for the SAT free of charge by visiting the College Board's official website (collegeboard.com), where you can take a free, full-length practice test, and receive a free skills report and detailed explanation for all test questions.

Finally! Anything and everything under the sun . . . free!

Money-conscious consumers should make a beeline for the Freecycle Network (freecycle.org), a nonprofit pipeline to freebies large and small. After clicking on the site, locate your community by clicking filling in your location on the home page, and sign up at no charge. As a member, you can check out listings of free stuff that runs the gamut from sofas and treadmills to blenders and cameras. It's up to the giver to decide who receives the items they want to recycle.

continued from page 43

Buy frozen blueberries in season.

When fresh blueberries are in season, that's the time to also buy the frozen variety. Grocers often mark down frozen blueberries—and other frozen fruits and vegetables—when they're in peak season.

Chill your flowers. If you're spending money on cut flowers, you want them to brighten your home for as long as possible. Trim the stems, change the water daily, and put them in the refrigerator when you're asleep or at work. They'll last longer.

Preserve the beauty. Some fresh-cut flowers come with a little packet of preservative to add to the water, but if yours didn't, make your own by putting 2 teaspoons of sugar and 1 teaspoon of bleach in a quart of lukewarm water. The flowers will last for many days longer.

Freezer

Keep it full. Stock your freezer with water-filled plastic jugs if it isn't full. The frozen jugs will make your freezer more efficient (and your energy money well spent). Plus, you'll always have fresh water in a power outage.

Frosting

Bag it, freeze it, squeeze it. Don't toss leftover frosting. Put it into a small, strong plastic bag and throw it in the freezer. Next time you need to decorate baked goods, defrost the bag, mix a little water with the frosting, cut a small opening in a corner of the bag, and use it like a professional cake decorator!

Frozen food

Flash-freeze some savings. Yes, frozen food can be more expensive than dishes you make yourself, but it's a bargain compared to takeout or restaurant meals. If you eat out once or twice a week, skipping the restaurant meals and eating a fancy frozen meal instead can easily save you $20.

Furnace

Stay in tune and save 10 percent. Get your furnace tuned up every two years. You can save about 10 percent on your heating bills if you maintain it correctly.

Filter out inefficiency. Keep your furnace running at maximum efficiency by changing the filter every two months, not once a season. Filters are cheap and easy to change—slip the old one out, slip the new one in. You can usually get a better deal if you buy them in multipacks at your local big-box store.

Furniture

Design your price. You may not be a professional designer, but you can still ask for the designer's discount—usually 10 to 15 percent off. If the answer is no, request free delivery or a free trial period for the piece you've selected.

Go for two instead of one. If you're shopping for a couch but could use a chair too, ask the salesperson what kind of deal you can get if you buy both. You may be able to score a worthwhile price break.

Gardening

Growing a garden these days has become more than the simple pleasure of working the soil. A vegetable or herb garden can make a significant difference to your food bill, and a package of perennial seeds will provide years of annual color! Gardeners in the know are attuned to tons of ways to do what they love without spending a fortune in seeds or plants, bending over in the hot sun, or canning for hours in the kitchen.

Plant in containers, eat what's fresh while it's fresh, and give away the rest—to your family, your neighbors, your church, or a local soup kitchen. A bag of seasonal homegrown veggies is a gift worth its weight in gold to a non-gardener. You can also plant other gardens that don't require you to find recipients.

Throw it in, watch it grow. Forget about pricey annuals, and, instead, plant what will give you years of pleasure. Two of our senior gardening experts agree that the bright blues and purples of *Nepeta* (otherwise known as catmint) and varying yellow hues of *Coreopsis* make a garden pop in the most persnickety of soil conditions. The best news is that all you have to do is sprinkle the seeds along the ground before a light rain, and you'll have color for years, without fuss.

The no-maintenance lawn. Wait! Don't kill that moss that's creeping across your lawn. Dig up the grass nearby and let the moss grow instead. Moss gardening is a steadily growing trend, because it's lush, velvety, and beautiful to walk on and look at, and it requires absolutely no mowing. All it needs is shade, a bit of moisture, and, ideally, poor-quality, acidic soil. The EPA estimates that the average suburban grassy lawn requires 10,000 gallons of water annually, while a moss lawn requires about 1 percent of that. Check out mossacres.com for tips on moss gardening and to buy a moss starter kit.

Buying secret

If you're serious about putting in a fruit garden, wait until the end of the season and buy all the plants you like at the local nursery, where they'll be going cheap. Ask for advice from the experts at the nursery on whether the plants can winter over in your climate zone when they're going in the ground so late in the growing season. Most plants can survive but may need special mulching or covering. And the upshot is that you'll have gotten a terrific deal on your garden, sometimes as much as 75 percent off!

Herbs for a song, with parsley, sage, rosemary, and thyme. An herb garden doesn't require quite the same commitment level as a vegetable garden. You don't need to work the soil as deeply or tend the herbs as much. But the results are delightful, colorful, and fragrant. Many herbs, such as chives and cilantro, bloom with bright flowers as the growing season progresses. And what could be nicer than walking through your herb plants in the evening, trailing your hands across the leaves to release the fragrance of a rosemary bush, a bed of peppermint, a tangle of delicate thyme, or a bunch of basil? And whether you make pounds of pesto or dry some sage to enrich your Thanksgiving stuffing, an herb garden can enrich your life all year.

continued on page 57

The 18 best ways to spend less on gas

The price of gas has gone up to $3.99! No, wait, that's $2.29! Hold on—now it's $4.35! Suddenly it comes down a dollar, and the next thing you now, it's up again! Prices are rising all around us for all kinds of daily items, but the cost of filling up at the pump seems to hurt the worst. Maybe it's because we're forced to stand and stare helplessly at the pump as the numbers fly by. Or maybe it's because we can't cut corners and substitute a less-expensive form of fuel or make our own version at home. Or maybe it's because a full tank of gas can cost more than $50, each and every visit! Whatever the reason, the only way we can take back some control of our fuel costs is to adopt gas-saving strategies for our cars. To get you started, here are some proven ones. Use these tips at the gas station, when maintaining your car (simply maintaining your car can improve mileage by 19 percent!), and every time you drive. You'll be amazed by how you can turn your hulking gas-guzzler into a genteel sipping machine.

1. **Use the Internet to fill up your car.** To find the lowest gas price in your neighborhood, go online to one of the gas-price comparison sites that have emerged recently, such as GasPriceWatch.com or FuelMeUp.com. Then just enter your ZIP code. It will tell you the current price of gas at most every station within a few miles of your home. You'll be amazed at how much difference there will be—the range can be as much as 20 cents per gallon! It's worth the effort—the best price isn't always at the same station.

2. **Get gas on the right day.** Gas prices are often a few pennies higher on weekends, due to all those people running errands and going on car trips. So get in the habit of filling your vehicle in the middle of the week, when prices are usually

lower. This is especially true before holiday weekends!

3. **Don't "top off" your tank.** Those little squirts of gas you try to add to your tank at the end of a  filling often end up staying in the hose. That means you've actually given away gas to the next user of your pump!

4. **Change your air filter.** Most anyone can do this; don't wait until you go to the repair shop. Clogged or dirty air filters can reduce gas mileage by as much as 10 percent.

5. **Don't get tired.** Under-inflated tires can reduce gas mileage by 10 percent or more. So, keep a tire-pressure gauge in your car, find a gas station that lets you fill your tires for free, and adjust your tire pressure every other fill-up.

6. **Tighten that cap.** Ask your mechanic to make sure your gas cap is in perfect shape next time you visit your repair shop. Close to 20 percent of cars have damaged or loose (or even missing!) gas caps—resulting in almost 150 million gallons of gas being vaporized annually. Loose gas caps will often set off your engine light, costing you even more at the mechanic.

7. **Drive, don't idle.** You may want to warm up your car on cold mornings by letting it idle, but you're not doing your car—or your wallet— any favors. Your car's engine warms up faster when you drive; idling wastes time and about a quarter of gas every 15 minutes. If your car struggles in the morning cold,

it probably means your engine needs a tune-up.

And in general, stop idling! If you're going to be at a standstill for 10 seconds or more—say, at the drive-thru lane at a fast-food joint or bank—it's better to cut the engine and do your business inside.

8. Always wear soft-soled shoes when driving. Your gas pedal responds differently to different types of shoes. If you have a heavy shoe, or a shoe that has a very hard sole, you naturally push harder on the gas pedal, speeding you up and wasting gas. Light shoes with soft, spongy soles make you drive slower (often, without your realizing it!). Seems trivial, but consistently calmer, slower driving can save you hundreds a year!

9. Follow the rule of three. That is, do your errands in batches of three or more. Nothing wastes gas like a cold drive to the store and back for a single item. And since modern cars don't become fully efficient until the engine is warmed up, drive to the furthest errand first and then work your way back—a series of short stop-and-start trips will never allow your car to reach maximum efficiency.

10. Park it where the sun doesn't shine. Every time you park in the sun, some of the gas in your tank is lost to evaporation. The savvy driver will find a shady spot to park, even in winter. And speaking of parking, always park so that you can pull forward rather than waste gas backing up. Over time, it really does make a difference.

11. Keep windows shut and air-conditioning off. Whenever weather allows, use only the heater or fan to keep air circulating in your car. Open windows and air-conditioning both reduce gas efficiency. If the fan just isn't enough, follow this rule: Open your windows at under 40 mph, and use air-conditioning above that level. At low speeds, you waste less gas from the air drag of an open window than you do by running the AC. Above 40 mph, air drag goes up, and so should your windows. Fan speed does not affect fuel economy. So if you use the air conditioner, blast it and then shut it off.

12. Don't forget: Slow and steady wins the race. Drivers can improve mileage by anywhere from 12 percent to 55 percent—it's true!—by following the speed limit and swearing off aggressive driving. Hard starts and hard stops are a terrible waste of gas. And try to anticipate traffic flow and avoid quickly accelerating or braking. For the very best fuel economy, avoid rapid acceleration and coast as long as you can into your stops, so they are always gentle and require minimal braking. Going over the speed limit cuts fuel economy as much as 23 percent. Put another way: Each 5 mph you drive over 60 is like paying an extra 15 cents a gallon. In addition, Edmunds.com found that using cruise control improves mileage by an additional 7 percent.

13. Follow the crowd. Avoid lonely gas stations in general and lonely gas stations off the highway in particular. They'll charge you more than gas stations at busy intersections or in bustling areas, where several are fighting to fill up your car.

14. Cruise to savings. Use cruise control and let the steady rate help improve your mileage by 7 percent (unless you're driving through lots of hills).

15. Get extra credit for filling up. Sign up for a credit card that gives you cash back for spending your hard-earned money at the gas pump. There are still a few cards out there that give you up to 5 percent back on gas and car maintenance costs.

16. Take the junk out of the trunk. Try to carry as light a load as possible in your car. Take out the shovel, the bags of salt, and any other heavy objects when you know you're not going to need them. You'll increase your fuel economy by decreasing your load.

17. Spend on maintenance; save on gas. Have your mechanic check for old spark plugs, dirty air filters, low fluid levels, and any other problems that may put a drag on your fuel economy. According to the Department of Energy, a well-maintained car can increase fuel efficiency by as much as 17 percent.

18. Avoid wealthy-neighborhood gas stations. Not only do gas stations in these places pass the higher costs of the land beneath them on to the customer, but also the local residents might be a little less price sensitive—so the gas stations are more likely to charge more for their gas.

continued from page 51

Cultivate a cutting garden. If you've only ever bought flowers from a store, you may be surprised at how easy it can be to grow a "cutting garden" of flowers. Hardy brown-eyed Susans or Michaelmas daisies, bright zinnias or snapdragons can grow in a season and be ready to fill vases, bouquets, and photographs by midsummer. Heavy-headed peonies or heirloom roses may take a year or more to establish before they start to bloom, but once they get started, they'll bring you joy for seasons to come.

The (new) Victory Garden. When food prices are as high as an elephant's eye, it's time to grow some food! A vegetable garden isn't expensive to begin, but it does require a fair amount of effort to turn the soil and break up the clumps; see if you can find a helpful neighbor with a tiller. Once you've dug your plot, it's easy and inexpensive to grow many, many veggies from seed, from beans and squash to pumpkins and lettuce. Other plants, such as tomatoes, are often best grown from bedding plants. If you've never planted a garden before, give it a try—nothing tastes as sweet as a pea you grew yourself!

Find your inner Johnny Appleseed. There are plenty of fruit trees and plants that will produce in a year or two—and blueberries are high on that list. Blueberries are now grown commercially in 38 states, so you've got a good chance of living in a climate that will support these luscious little jewels. Invest in a couple of blueberry bushes at a local nursery, and you may find yourself making blueberry pancakes and muffins with

continued on page 64

The 10 golden rules of grocery shopping

Does grocery shopping seem like a chore? It doesn't have to be! Think of it as a game instead, and you'll find that you can have fun on your next outing—and you'll save tons of money at the same time. Just like any game, though, grocery shopping requires a bit of strategy. Just follow these 10 rules, and you'll always walk away a winner.

GOLDEN RULE #1:
READ GROCERY ADS BEFORE SHOPPING.

Like so many other retailers, grocery stores constantly have popular products on sale as a way to lure you into the store. And to get the word out, they advertise a lot—through mailings to your house, inserts in newspapers and local shopping guides, commercials on TV or the radio, and sometimes even online. They are worth studying each and every week! That's because what is on sale changes on a weekly basis. Knowing that lettuce is on sale, you might map out menus that focus on that ingredient: For example, use lettuce for a mixed salad one day, for topping a taco the next day, and to wrap chicken for a low-carb dish the next.

Building your menu around sales items will save you a fortune over time.

GOLDEN RULE #2:
NAVIGATE THE STORE LIKE A PRO.

The most successful money-saving shoppers are those who approach the grocery store with a solid game plan. Here are some of their secrets:

Make a beeline for the back of the market. Ever notice how the milk department is at the very back of the store? That's no accident—supermarket layouts are designed such that you have to walk by all the nice-to-have snack and gourmet foods before you get to essentials like milk, bread, and eggs. Make a beeline to the back of the store, and try to avoid the tempting center aisles.

Shop the perimeter of the store. Food essentials (produce, meats, dairy, and bread) are usually located around the store's perimeter. The middle aisles

have the more costly prepared foods. The more you concentrate your shopping on the edges of the store, the healthier and cheaper your food-buying will be.

Be familiar with your grocer's aisles. Every store has an aisle or two that has no temptations for you (pet food, paper goods, baby supplies, cosmetics, and so forth). Make that aisle your passageway to the departments you need at the back of the store. Why tempt yourself by walking down the candy aisle?

Shop the middle of the aisle. Food companies pay big money for grocery stores to place their products prominently on the ends of aisles (also called "endcaps"), where you can't help but see them. Sometimes these endcaps display genuinely good deals on

nonessential products, but pantry staples are usually smack-dab in the middle of the aisles. Grocers reason that you'll seek out the staples you really need, and in so doing, you'll have to pass (twice!) all the extras they want you to buy. Look up, look down, look all around. Generally, the most expensive brand-name items are on shelves at eye level. Less expensive store brands are on the upper and lower shelves.

GOLDEN RULE #3: GET ORGANIZED!

With grocery store sales in mind, make a list of what you need to buy and stick to it. If you shop on Sundays, for example, make decisions on what you'll have for dinner Monday through Friday. Your shopping list should include all the food you'll need for those dinners, plus fruit, yogurt, milk, eggs, and bread for breakfasts, and whatever food you need for lunches or snacks. Weed out expired coupons and put new coupons into their appropriate slots in your coupon organizer. Make sure your store loyalty cards, rain checks, and a calculator are in your wallet, and you're ready to go. By being this organized, you not only make fewer trips to the grocery store, but also end up throwing out less food.

GOLDEN RULE #4: DO THE MATH.

Calculate the savings. One bag of chips is $1.49, and a seemingly same-size bag is $1.79. The cheaper one is the better deal, right? Not necessarily, if in reality, the higher priced bag has a couple more ounces of chips. When comparing prices at the store, always compare price per pound (or per ounce or pint, for liquids). It's the only objective way to compare costs. Most stores put that number in the small print of the product shelf tags; get used to comparing those numbers, not the total price. And keep a calculator with you (or use the one on your smartphone)—it makes comparison shopping a breeze.

GOLDEN RULE #5: STUDY YOUR STORE'S SELLING PATTERNS FOR SALES.

Grocery store sales often occur in patterns. For example, we know of a grocery store that puts our favorite ice cream on a "buy one, get one free" sale on the third week every month. On the first week of the month, it's only a dollar off. Learn the patterns (and keep track of them in a notebook). Hold off buying these items until you know that they'll be at their rock-bottom prices—then buy enough of it to last you until the great sale is run again. By learning these cycles and adjusting your purchasing habits to them, you can guarantee never paying full price for many of your favorite staples.

GOLDEN RULE #6: LEARN THE TRICKS OF THEIR TRADE.

Here's a well-kept secret: When a grocery store advertises a special—say, buy ten containers of yogurt for $5—you don't have to buy the number of items they're advertising. In this case, you could buy one container for 50 cents. Unless the store specifically states otherwise, you should buy as few as you want.

Here's another: Sometimes it's hard to find handheld grocery baskets—they are usually tucked into a corner at the store's entrance. You feel like a cart is your only option, and that's what the grocers want. Once you have a cart, they reason, you won't even think twice while filling it up. If you only need a few things, seek out the baskets . . . and stick to that shopping list!

GOLDEN RULE #7:
USE COUPONS (WISELY).

Remember all those articles about women who go grocery shopping and get $300 worth of groceries for $2.67? They have many tricks up their sleeves, but their biggest trick is using coupons. Here are proven strategies for following this golden rule.

Read more, save more. If your Sunday newspaper offers a high-value coupon on an item that you buy often, it may be worth the cost to buy extra copies of the paper for the extra coupons, or to ask neighbors if you can have the coupon inserts from their papers. This is particularly worthwhile if you know that an item you want is a "buy one, get one free" sale; you can then get four for the price of two and have ample supplies in your pantry.

Trade and save. Have friends or family that you know use coupons? Offer to host a twice-a-month coupon-trading session over coffee. Even better, do your "swapping" long-distance over the phone, and then send friends and family their coupons through the mail. That way, the mix of coupons will be wider—the types of coupons on offer (and the coupons' savings amounts) vary by region.

Go online to save. More and more websites are offering coupons you can print out. Before you go shopping, log on to the Internet and, in your favorite search engine, put in the name of a product on your shopping list, plus the word "coupon." Chances are better than not that deals will pop up. Just be careful—some sites want lots of personal information in exchange for access to coupons or discounts. Read the fine print and be sure it is a reputable website before surrendering personal information.

Sort smartly. Organize your coupons the way you organize your shopping list: in the same order as the store aisles. Some people use a plain envelope, some people use recipe boxes with dividers—find the way that works best for you. If you are organized, you'll find the coupons you want more quickly and will be less likely to overlook a useful one. As you clip them, put each coupon in a product category. Within each category, put them in expiration order, putting the ones closest to expiration on top.

Seek out stores that double or triple coupons. Some grocers double coupons up to $1 in face value; others triple coupons regularly (or on certain days of the week).

Know when small packages can yield the biggest discounts. Buying the largest size of most items is usually the thriftiest option, but calculating bargains might work out differently when using coupons (especially "two-fer" coupons that require you to buy two of the same item to get your discount). Using a coupon and buying two smaller-size items may yield you a better price per pound.

GOLDEN RULE #8: SAVE RAIN CHECKS FOR A RAINY DAY.

This rule works best when you shop at a popular, high-volume grocery store: Say the sales circulars come out on Thursdays for sales that begin on Friday. There's a great deal on 12-packs of cola, but you don't have the money (or the space) to stock up on it this week. If you go shopping on Saturday or Sunday, these sale items are

probably already out of stock. Good—that's exactly what you want. Ask for a rain check on the sold-out bargains, and you can cash in on those sales when it's convenient for you.

GOLDEN RULE #9:
LAYER, LAYER, LAYER.

Use a manufacturer's coupon with items already on sale at the grocery store. Some people call this "layering," others call it "stacking"— but it's really a simple way of "saving!" Say a $1.99 package of taco shells is on sale for $1.49. If you have a 50-cents-off coupon and the store doubles coupons, you'll only pay 49 cents for it!

GOLDEN RULE #10:
WATCH THE REGISTER.

You've probably seen those investigative shows that uncover just how many errors supermarket scanners make—the numbers are staggering. Knowing this, keep a watchful eye on the cashier's display as the cashier scans each product. Make sure that discounts for sales and coupons are applied. Make sure that the clerk keys in the proper produce codes for perishables without price tags, so that you're not paying for exotic mushrooms when you're buying green peppers. And make sure that the register is logging items with price tags correctly—when there's a mistake, many stores give you the product for free when you point out their errors.

And after you've confirmed that your purchase was correctly tabulated, be sure to keep your receipt. This is a good practice for a few reasons: If the item is on sale but doesn't ring up with the sales price, you can bring the receipt back to the store for a refund. (Some stores may refund you the difference if that grocery item is on sale at a competing store, too.) If you get home and find out that one of your items is damaged or has a broken seal, you can easily return it. Finally, many register tapes are printed with valuable local coupons on the reverse side. Read carefully and keep saving!

continued from page 57

your own supply before summer is out. You can also find apple, pear, and peach trees of medium size that will produce by the following season—just be sure to plant more than one for cross-pollination, and be sure to keep a close eye out for pests.

Garden gloves

Clean, not green. Buy an inexpensive pair of cloth gardening gloves to cut down on cleaning costs. Use them to wipe dust and dirt from window blinds and shutters. Unlike expensive cleaning wipes, you can toss them in the laundry and use them again and again.

Gifts

Become a fan to get a fan. A great inexpensive gift for a child who's also a sports fan: a fan-mail package from his or her favorite sports team. Some packages are free, some cost up to $15 (depending on the team), and most contain a crowd-pleasing assortment of items such as bumper stickers, magnets, team photos, and more. Check out the website of your favorite team for ordering info.

Keep it in the family. Here's a gift idea that will thrill all your relatives, as well as your wallet. Gather favorite recipes, copy them, and create a family cookbook for everyone in your family.

Give a gift certificate—from you. Give a friend or family member a gift of your time. Whether the recipient needs babysitting, cooking, snow shoveling, or gardening, use your talents and your time to give a welcome (and inexpensive) present.

Celebrate Christmas all year. Buy half-price gifts after Christmas, and give them at birthdays, anniversaries, and so on. You can also buy holiday gift sets at bargain prices, take them apart, and either give the gifts separately or repackage them for the appropriate occasion.

The gift of practicality. If you're on a budget and don't know what to give as a gift, choose an inexpensive practical gift that anyone would appreciate. Stamps, stationery, pens, cookies, coffee, and other simple, useful, and expendable gifts are particularly welcomed by those who don't have a lot of space.

Don't go empty-handed (or with an empty wallet). Holiday parties are great fun, but they can get expensive if you take a gift to each one. Save on hostess gifts by buying thoughtful presents in bulk: cocktail napkins, bars of scented soap, pretty candles, and so on.

The perfect photo-op. Give grandchildren inexpensively framed photos of their parents at the recipient's current age—the goofier, the better. You'll provide laughs and memories for everyone at a picture-perfect price.

Greeting cards

Send sentiments for less. Forget about buying traditional greeting cards at the stationery store. Instead, buy packages of greeting cards (either all-occasion or blank) at your warehouse club, craft store, discount store, or mass-merchandiser. At $2.29 per individual card, you can save around $10 by buying a multi-card package. You'll also save on gas by not running out to get a card every time you need one.

Make sentiments for nothing. Collect bits of scrap paper, fabric, clipped-out pictures from magazines—the sky's the limit—and make your own greeting cards. The effort will not only be appreciated, but it might also be framed!

It's like printing money. If you have a color printer, design and print your own gift cards, either with a simple word-processing program, or with a special paper and software package that offers you hundreds of designs and styles to make each card your own, available at stationery stores.

Groceries

Bag it. Save money and the environment by bringing your own bags to the grocery store. More and more stores are giving you money back for every bag you reuse.

Weigh in on savings. Whenever you buy potatoes or onions or any other produce by the bag rather than by the pound, weigh several bags and buy the heaviest one. You may get a 10½-pound bag for the price of the 10-pound bag.

When old is new again. Don't fall for food described as "featured" in the aisles of your grocery store. The manager may just be promoting a commonly found food at its regular price.

Don't fall for limits. Keep your money in your purse when you see signs like "Limit six per customer." Stores know that customers will buy more of an item if they think there's a shortage—and there generally isn't.

Double up. Try to stretch out the time between grocery-shopping trips. Instead of going once a week, go once every two weeks. You'll be forced to make your current food last longer and use up the food sitting patiently in the pantry and freezer.

Hair color

Lengthen the color of your locks. Stretch out appointments for hair colorings or touch-ups by using a shampoo designed for color-treated hair. The color-enhancing shampoo won't cost much more than your regular shampoo, and it can easily save you $100 per year on colorings.

Don't stray too far. Be sure to stay within two shades of your natural hair color when you visit the salon. Your roots will blend into the colored hair better when it grows out, allowing more time between colorings.

Haircuts

Return to school. Head to the nearest beauty school or salon training facility to get a salon-style haircut (and color) at a barbershop price. A supervised stylist-in-training will cut your hair; you'll cut the cost of an ongoing expense. Visit beautyschoolsdirectory.com to find a school near you.

Alternate and save. Can't give up your pricey haircuts? Consider alternating appointments at your usual salon with visits to a less expensive one, where you can get maintenance cuts for a fraction of what you normally pay.

Cut down on your cuts. If you can't give up your expensive stylist, try stretching out the time between trips to the salon. Instead of getting a cut every four weeks, aim for every five and save the cost of three visits per year.

Trim your costs. If all you need is an easy trim, head over to a barbershop instead of your usual salon. You shouldn't have trouble finding a cut for under $20.

Try something new. Or at least try a new salon. Many salons just starting out need new customers, and they often offer deals for haircuts. You can save up to 50 percent on a haircut in a brand-new salon.

Save up to $20 by saying no. Whether you're getting your hair cut or colored, skip the blow-dry. Salons often charge big-time for drying your hair, so tell them not to. Keep the $20 in your pocket.

Hangers

Hang on to your hangers. Don't toss out a good hanger just because it has rough edges. Dab a little clear nail polish on the rough spot, and it's ready to go back to work.

Hospitals

Pack a bag. Try to bring toothpaste, aspirin, tissues, and other necessities from home next time you head to the hospital. You will be amazed by how much the hospital will charge you for such ordinary items.

Check your bill. Hospitals have been known to charge patients for procedures they never received, rooms never used, and medicine never administered. Check your hospital bill carefully, and question anything that doesn't look right.

continued on page 84

Holidays made easy
Smart tactics for thrifty and fun gift buying

Holiday gift shopping: Do the words terrify you, or make your eyes light up with anticipation? Either way, we have advice to make holiday shopping easier, cheaper, less stressful, and more fun. But before you read our savvy hints and tips, take a minute to remember why you're shopping. Chances are, it's about the pleasure in giving those you love gifts that truly express your feelings for them. Remember that—it'll make all the hunting and haggling more than worth it.

BEFORE YOU GO

Before the search for the "perfect" gift begins, there are a few things to consider. Mainly: Who? What? How much? And when?

1. **Set a limit.** Giving gifts should fill your heart, not empty your savings account. If setting a budget seems more bother than it's worth, at least determine an approximate figure ($25 to $75 for family, $15 to $25 for friends) for each person on your list.

2. **Record gift ideas.** Smart gift-givers know that gathering should happen 12 months of the year. So buy a notebook, attach a pen, and keep track of whom you need to buy gifts for, and ideas you get from window-shopping, catalog browsing, or just sudden inspirations that pop into your mind. Then, when you do buy a gift for someone, mark it down as well.

3. **Clip pictures or ads.** Holiday season is catalog season, but most of us get catalogs year-round, too. Don't toss them in the recycling bin. Look for ideas. When you see something that seems right for someone, clip out the picture and description, note the person's name and the catalog, and file it away for future use.

4. **Think about whom you're buying for.** In that same

notebook, include information about each person, such as sizes, interests, sports, and hobbies. Even add gifts you've given in the past, so you don't accidentally duplicate.

5. **Be an off-peak shopper.** Unless you enjoy packed parking lots, messy stores, huge crowds, over-warm stores, and surly clerks, skip shopping on the six or so weekends that lead up to Christmas. Instead, shop weekday mornings or early afternoons. Not only will the crowds be smaller, but the stores will also be neatened up and restocked.

6. **Dress comfortably.** Serious holiday shopping is not the time for high fashion. Wear loose-fitting clothes, tie your hair back or, at a minimum, wear comfortable shoes so you can navigate crowds and stand in long lines without discomfort. And to avoid energy lags and endless time in food courts, have a good meal before heading out to the stores.

SUREFIRE SHOPPING STRATEGIES

You've followed our advice above and are ready for business! Here's what you can do to make your shopping excursion a productive one, without breaking the bank:

7. **Always, always use a shopping list.** Random, unfocused shopping leads to impulse buying, overspending, and forgetting gifts for certain people. And that means having to go shopping again.

8. **Shop year-round.** No, this doesn't mean that you're

Create a gift stash.

The good part of gift shopping year-round is that you minimize shopping craziness in the busiest retail season of the year. The challenging part of year-round shopping: finding a place to store it all. Here's what you do:

✔ Find a closet shelf, dresser drawer, trunk, or cupboard, and designate this as your "stash" area. Whenever you see that perfect something—and it's worth the cost—buy it, even if it's January. When you get home, carefully add a note to the item, listing when and where you bought it, whom it is for, and how much you spent.

✔ If you buy gift items that aren't for anyone in particular, store them separately. Keep a clipboard with the stash and write in all the items available for usage. The next time you have a birthday, anniversary, shower, or other gift-giving occasion, check the clipboard before shopping. You might already have the perfect item!

✔ This is also a good place to put gifts given to you that you either already have or cannot use. Just be sure to attach a sticky note with the gift giver's name, so you don't give it back to that person.

constantly shopping. It means that you are always looking. Because you never know when you might see the absolute perfect gift (at a deal, no less) for someone. And just because you got a great gift for $20 on a discount in March, doesn't mean you need to spend more to bring it up to the originally budgeted cost. Gift giving is about the thought, not money.

9. **Shop on vacation.** If you go somewhere on vacation, watch out for things that might make someone else happy come Christmastime. Going to a new city or country can open up shopping opportunities that don't usually exist for you.

10. **Stay current with the business news.** Holiday retail sales are a huge part of the American economy, so the media covers the action in great detail. By following the business news, you'll learn about who is discounting, what's hot and what's not, what products are in surplus or short supply, and who is offering unusual deals. Use

all this information to help strategize when and where to shop for best prices and selection.

11. **Don't be afraid to haggle.** It can pay to be bold. Ask a manager: "Is this item going on sale soon?" "Is this the best price you can offer?" or "Are there any discounts for loyal customers?" The worst they can say is "no." But you may be surprised at how many stores consider your request.

12. **Go with gift cards.** Sure, they might not give you the warm fuzzies, but giving people the opportunity to choose what they want is never a bad thing. If you want to be distinctive, offer a certificate to an out-of-the-ordinary place, such as a French bakery, high-end restaurant, or day spa. Make

sure you read the "fine print" to learn about hidden charges or expiration dates.

SAVVY ONLINE SHOPPING

Maybe you've had enough of long lines or can't justify how much it costs to drive to the mall! If that's true, you're probably shopping the Internet. After all, what's not to love about those online bargains and convenience? Make your Web experience a wonderful one with these tips:

13. **Search for sales.** Some online retailers have sales like those at brick-and-mortar stores, with lots of promotion around the event. But even if there is no announced sale, many retailer sites have a permanent discount "room" with nicely marked-down products. Search your favorite online stores for these secret savings.

14. **Compare prices.** You found the perfect baseball mitt for your son on a national sporting-good chain's website. Don't order yet! Write down the name and model number,

and do a search of the item on your favorite search engine with the added words "best price." You'll not only find other vendors that sell that item (at varying costs), but you'll also often run across reviews of the product and online retailer.

15. Factor in shipping. Each website has its own shipping charges. And some do a good job of hiding it! Never make a purchase without understanding the full costs involved. A $49.95 item is a better bargain with free shipping than the same item marked down to $39.95 but with $14.95 for shipping.

16. Save all paperwork! When you place an online order, print the confirmation page, which includes the total sale, product information, and confirmation number. Also, when items arrive, file the invoice and any other papers (like return forms and envelopes) in a well-organized folder or binder.

17. Shop at off-peak hours. While larger sites have the capacity to handle lots of e-shoppers, smaller sites struggle with online crowds. Find a time when there are fewer people searching the Web, such as late nights, early mornings, and Sundays.

18. Check for good affiliations. High-quality online retailers use well-known, national organizations for billing, quality control, consumer support, or merely to show that they are legitimate and safe. Look at the bottom of the home page of the website to see if it carries such logos as PayPal, Bizrate.com, BBB Online, or Shopping.com Trusted Store.

19. Get other's opinions. Several websites not only find you the best price of a product but also give you consumer ratings and comments on the online stores selling the product. If you aren't certain about a website's quality, seek out consumer comments at price-comparison websites like nextag.com.

Something for everyone

Be honest. No matter how much planning you've done, there's always someone who pops up at the last minute. Go ahead . . . use these imaginative gift ideas (we don't care if you take the credit).

✔ **For the animal-lover,** buy a festive dog or cat food bowl, fill it with tasty tidbits, add a small toy, and wrap it up.

✔ **For the writer,** pick up a basket and fill it with handsome pens, note cards, a journal, handmade paper, and rubber stamps or decorative stickers.

✔ **For the nature-lover,** pair up a bird field guide and binoculars or a feeder. Campers will appreciate a book of local trail maps or basket filled with graham crackers, marshmallows, good-quality chocolate bars, and toasting forks for s'mores.

✔ **For the gardener,** buy or paint a pretty planter and fill it with seed packets of heirloom flowers, vegetables, or herbs, some copper plant markers, and a trowel.

✔ **For the gourmet,** find a breadbasket and fill it with flavored oils and vinegars, dipping sauces, or spices. Or pack a rustic crate with fresh produce like apples, pears, or citrus, cider, pies or cakes, and gourmet nuts and jams.

✔ **For the romantic**, give a basket with a bottle of wine or champagne, dried pasta and sauce, pastries, and a candle. A gift certificate to a restaurant and movie passes work well, too.

✔ **For the sports-lover,** try golf lessons or a basket of golf balls, tees, or fun club-head cover. Or give tickets to their favorite sporting events or a gift card to the best sports bar in town.

20. Beware of the dangers.
While most sites are safe, there are things you can do to protect yourself. For example, look at the address of the website's order page: It should start with "https." That extra "s" at the end of "http" means it is a secure connection. Also, don't give out Social Security numbers, bank account data, or any passwords other than the one you might have registered with that one site. The only personal data to give is your

credit card number—and yes, do buy products with a credit card! It's generally quite safe, and you have protection under the federal Fair Credit Billing Act if something goes wrong.

BEYOND GIFTS

For those people "who have everything," or for those loved ones in which another wrapped box just doesn't say what's in your heart, here are ideas for gifts that are truly individual and special.

21. Consider giving an event. Each of us has our passions; why not let your loved ones engage in theirs? Buy them tickets to the opera, play, circus, football game, concert, or lecture that they most would enjoy seeing or hearing. Or, if they love food, reserve a table for two (or the family) at the restaurant they always dreamed of trying but never got to. A magical evening out is often more memorable than one more necktie or kitchen appliance, after all.

22. Consider giving a membership. What gardener wouldn't love a year's membership to the local botanical garden? What art-lover wouldn't be happy with a membership to the art museum? All kinds of memberships are available with wonderful benefits, be they free admissions, a monthly magazine, or access to online services not available to others.

23. Give of yourself. Sometimes, the best gift of all is *you*. Give a handwritten coupon, to be redeemed over the coming year, for home-cooked meals, a visit, a weekend away, a personal car wash, even a massage. Better yet, give a coupon book with a mix of offers, large and small. Sometimes, the best gift you can give costs no money at all.

IT'S A WRAP

When it comes to gift giving, the outside is just as important as the inside. A uniquely wrapped present makes a statement that you care, that your gift is special, and that you're offering more than just an object. It shows you're giving your time and creativity as well. But here's a little secret—a great wrapped gift doesn't have to take any more time than an ordinary one. All you need is a few basics to turn dozens of plain presents into amazing pieces of art.

If you're in a hurry or overly stressed, using purchased wrapping paper, premade bows, and square boxes is the way to go. But if you want to go "outside the box" to creative gift wrapping, you'll need the right supplies and tools. Keep in mind that you don't need everything on this list if you're just getting started. Instead, grow your supplies over time.

24. Buy a variety of paper.

Purchase gift wrap in a wide range of colors, patterns, and finishes. Also get both white and colored tissue paper, brown craft paper, construction paper, corrugated paper, and crepe paper. Consider specially finished paper such as marbled or foil, handmade paper, and transparent paper, such as cellophane or tracing papers.

25. Consider using fabrics.

Any family that has a sewer probably has lots of extra fabric sitting around in bins, going unused. Use the fabric for wrapping! Good types include silk, printed cotton, muslin, and velvet, velveteen, or velour. You may also need taffeta and netting.

26. Say it with paint.
Painting words or designs on wrapping paper or boxes can be both fun and personal. Buy ready-to-use poster or gouache paint, spray paint, and specialty acrylic paints. You'll also want a variety of paintbrushes, from tiny detail brushes to wider ones. Also get sponge brushes and natural sponges for stamping patterns.

27. Time to get sticky.
Tapes and adhesives you need include clear cellophane tape, double-sided tape, masking tape,

painter's tape, white glue, tacky glue, glue dots, and glitter glue.

28. **Cut it up.** The most important cutting tool is scissors. You'll want both straight-edged and decorative- or scalloped-edged, medium to large, and at least one pair of small, pointed scissors for fine work. Hole punches and a utility or craft knife also are handy to have.

29. **Tie it up right.** Ribbons, ties, and bows come in a variety of shapes and sizes. Some to consider are fabric ribbon, wire-edged ribbon, flat and self-curling paper and synthetic ribbon, twisted paper ribbon, grosgrain ribbon, raffia, pre-tied bows, plain and decorative string, yarns, and embroidery threads.

30. **Gather finishing flourishes.** Other decorative items you might consider using include stickers, confetti, flat sequins or flat-backed jewels, pom-poms, pipe cleaners, beads, buttons, and dried or silk flowers, leaves, or fruit. Finally, don't forget to use stencils and stamps to add to your design, too.

CHALLENGING ITEMS TO WRAP

Boxes are pretty straightforward to wrap, but there are some shapes and sizes that present a greater challenge.

31. **Round items.** These require a covering that will mold itself to a sphere. Good paper choices include crepe, tissue, foil, or cellophane. Just about any fabric will do the trick, so let the gift and the occasion determine the type of fabric used.

32. **Bottles.** These go best in bought or homemade gift bags. Wrapping a bottle in a swath of fabric or soft paper, such as crepe or tissue paper also works well. To create a cylindrical box for a bottle, lay corrugated paper smooth side up on a flat surface and wrap the paper around the bottle tightly, securing it with strong double-sided tape or glue.

33. Odd shapes. You can place odd-shaped items in a gift bag or large box, but you can also be creative. If you're giving a hammer, for example, place its head between two paper plates and staple them together. Then use crepe paper to wrap the "lollipop" top, and wind ribbon around the "stick."

34. Extra-large gifts. You can buy gift bags for items like bicycles or exercise equipment, but you can also easily drape them with a festive tablecloth or sheet. Add a big bow and decorative extras.

SPECIAL WRAPPING EFFECTS

The style you lend to your gift wrapping can either be inspired by the gift itself or your decorating theme for the season.

35. Make it rustic. For a rustic look, use brown craft paper or butcher paper, either plain or sponge painted, stenciled, or stamped. Tie with simple twine, raffia, or neutral-colored grosgrain ribbons. Add tags made from cream-colored card stock, and tuck a sprig of pine, holly, or dried leaves in the bow.

36. Go a little bit country. To make a country-style present, wrap it in simple checked fabric, gingham, or plaid in seasonal colors, or matte-finished paper in dark red or dark green, or a patchwork of printed "calico" papers. Tie with gingham ribbon or yarn, and tuck a sprig of herbs or dried flowers plus a few cinnamon sticks in the bow.

37. Concoct a Victorian fantasy. Use rich fabrics, such as velvet and silk, floral chintz, or shiny brocades, or use heavy printed or embossed papers with a Victorian motif. Tie with lace or silk ribbons, or gold or silver cords, and make a tussie-mussie (form a cone from a piece of lace or a doily, and fill it with silk or dried flowers) and attach it at the bow.

A child's special touch

If you still have young ones (or even slightly older ones) at home, making your own gift wrap can be a fun family project.

1. Start with rolls of butcher paper or brown craft paper. Spread a plastic tarp over a large flat surface (we prefer the floor) and make sure everyone dresses in old clothes.

2. Bring out rubber stamps and ink pads, simple stencils and poster paints, potatoes for block prints, crayons, marking pens, watercolors, colored chalks (and a spray fixative to prevent smearing the final product), stickers, and whatever else inspires you.

3. Let the family go to town. You can collaborate or give each person his or her own paper to decorate. This will result in truly unique, heartfelt gift wrap—one that most grandparents will cherish as much as the gift inside.

38. Design an ethnic masterpiece. To give a present an ethnic flavor, use the colors of the culture's flags. A world atlas is invaluable to carry out this theme.

39. Take a chance with color. Add real flair to your wrappings with saturated color. Though red and green are traditional colors, this year expand your vision and use a selection of deep saturated colors in papers or fabrics. Rich eggplant purple, midnight blue, brilliant tangerine orange, chocolate brown, hot pink, turquoise, plum—be open to new colors.

GOING BEYOND THE BOX

Square and rectangle boxes are inevitable, but open your eyes and look around. There are other wonderful ways to conceal a present.

40. Use old hatboxes. Often covered with decorative paper and coming in all sizes, these are generally round (though some can be octagonal) and have their own carrying cords. Look for them in craft stores, resale shops, thrift shops, and garage sales. With very little effort, you can turn these into collectible containers for your gifts.

41. Don't forget decorative tins. These have experienced a resurgence of popularity and are now readily available in all sizes and shapes. Look for shining new tins and antique reproductions, or haunt antique stores, thrift shops, and flea markets for authentic historic tins.

42. Make a creative crate. Running the gamut from exquisitely finished and polished pieces to right-off-the-back-of-the-wagon rustic, wooden crates and boxes are eye-catchers. So save those clementine boxes for future gift giving!

43. Try wooden cheese boxes. A bit harder to come by, these are similar to hat boxes in their roundness and having a separate lid, but they are made of wood, and some can be really

extraordinary. Leave these undecorated so the beauty of the wood shines, and tie up with raffia, twine, or simple grosgrain ribbons.

44. Roll out the barrel. Take a trip back to the old general store, where many goods were shipped and displayed in wooden barrels. Old nail kegs and small liquor barrels can conceal fairly big gifts. They are also terrific to keep afterward for planters or for storing long-handled gardening tools or umbrellas.

GIFT-INSPIRED WRAPPING

Another way to approach gift wrapping is to let the kind of gift—and the interests of the recipient—inspire the kind of wrapping, so that it becomes a part of the present.

45. A baby. Wrap a large gift in a baby's blanket and a small gift in a cloth diaper or burping cloth. Fasten with diaper pins and decorate with small baby toys, such as a set of plastic keys or a wooden teething toy.

46. **A cook.** Wrap a gift for a cook in tea towels or appliance covers, fasten with kitchen twine, and decorate with a set of measuring spoons, a melon baller, a wooden spoon crossed with a rubber spatula, or cookie cutters.

47. **A book-lover.** For someone who loves to read, wrap a special book in a fabric book cover and decorate the bow with a special bookmark or book light.

48. **A wine-lover.** Choose a good bottle of wine, then set it in a wine cooler, tie a ribbon around the top and decorate with a corkscrew, decorative cork, or glass charms.

49. **A woman.** Wrap lingerie, perfume, or jewelry for a woman in a large silk scarf, gather the corners together to form a bag, tie with a satin ribbon, and decorate with a small sachet.

50. **A man.** Wrap smaller presents in bandannas or white handkerchiefs, and larger presents in a blue work shirt, flannel plaid shirt, or beloved sports team T-shirt. Decorate according to his interests.

CREATIVE GIFT TAGS

The final touch on a well-wrapped package is, of course, a gift tag. Sure, store-bought tags do the trick, but you'll have more fun designing your own.

51. **Get it done with paper.** For paper tags, use a good, solid paper, card stock, or thin cardboard as the base. Cut out seasonal shapes (stars, holly leaves, Christmas trees, stockings, wreaths, candy canes, and so on) or geometric shapes. Then paint, gild, stamp, or decorate with colored pens or crayons.

Easier yet: Cut fun shapes out of boldly colored or patterned wrapping paper.

52. **Pick your fabric.** To make fabric tags, begin with fairly sturdy fabric (brocades, felt, heavy-duty cotton, or duck cloth). Cut out the shape desired and seal the edges with glue or a product made to prevent raveling (sold at craft and fabric stores). Use fabric pens to decorate and write names on the tags, and then attach them to the bows on the package using embroidery thread, yarn, thin cording, or thin ribbons.

53. **Make it with dough.** This is a wonderfully fun and creative way to create personalized, hardened gift tags. Combine ½ cup table salt with ½ cup water in a saucepan, and bring the mixture to a boil. Meanwhile, mix ½ cup cold water with ½ cup cornstarch in a bowl. Add the cornstarch mixture to the boiling salt water and stir vigorously to prevent it from lumping. Reduce the heat to low and cook, stirring constantly, until the mixture is stiff. Remove the saucepan from the heat and, using a large spoon, carefully turn the mixture onto a wooden cutting board. Let the mixture cool. Knead the mixture until it is smooth, and then roll out to a ¼-inch thickness. Using floured cookie cutters, cut out as many shapes as desired. Transfer the shapes to baking sheets, use a straw to poke holes at the top of each shape, and bake in a 200°F oven for 2 hours. Cool the shapes on wire racks. Paint or decorate as desired, and tie the tags to boxes threading cord, ribbon, or string through the holes in the tops.

continued from page 69

Wait for your surgery. Ask to be admitted to the hospital on the day of your surgery, not before—you'll pay dearly for that extra day. Early admission generally benefits the staff, not you or your hospital bill.

Don't take the same test twice. Make sure your doctor sends all test results to the hospital so you won't be subjected to the same procedures again. You'll save money—and a lot of aggravation.

Free health care. Hospitals frequently offer skin-cancer screenings, cholesterol tests, wellness seminars, and other services as a way to connect with their local community. Call your nearby hospital to find out what kinds of services they offer for free.

Hotels

Make it like home. Hotels can be expensive, and eating out only adds to the cost of your vacation. The next time you book a hotel, ask for a room that includes a kitchen. This may mean spending more on a suite, but once you factor in the cost of three meals a day at restaurants, it will also mean big savings—probably more than $50 a day. Try an extended-stay hotel for a good deal on a suite.

Call the hotel directly. You may save money on a phone call by dialing a hotel's toll-free number, but you may save a lot more on your hotel room by calling the hotel directly. Staffers at the hotel generally have more flexibility in giving discounts on room rates than those at the central reservations number, and they may be able to give you a better price than the main reservation line offers.

Choose a business hotel for a leisure stay. Many fancy chain hotels that cater to business travelers find themselves with empty rooms on the weekends. They often drop their rates to entice customers. Call one of them for a good weekend deal.

Look beyond the room for savings. Just because you got a great deal on a hotel room doesn't mean you got the best deal. You need to look for the hotel's additional money-saving features. Does your room have a small refrigerator? Does the rate include free breakfast? Does the hotel offer free parking? A free Wi-Fi connection? Factor in these freebies when you choose your hotel, and your good deal will look great.

House buying

Time it right. Shop for a house in the dead of winter when other home buyers are staying home. (If you live in the Sunbelt, shop in the heat of the summer for the same reason.) Even in a buyer's market, the time of year can make a big difference. Your off-season timing may just knock a hefty percentage off the in-season price.

Housekeeping

It bears repeating. Never spend money again on expensive household cleaners. Save yourself money over and over by substituting a simple 1-to-1 solution of white vinegar and water in a spray bottle for commercial cleaning products. You'll never buy the other stuff again. You'll be green, and your home will be clean as a whistle.

Ice cream

Free ice cream. One day, once a year, most Ben & Jerry's stores worldwide give away free ice-cream cones. All free, all day, no limit. Check out benjerry.com to find out the specific day and the location of a store near you. If it's your birthday (and you can prove it), Baskin-Robbins will give you a free 2.5-ounce scoop, no matter what your age.

Ice pack

Freeze your costs. Do you need an ice pack for muscle aches and pains? Don't bother spending your money on the drugstore kind. Instead, make a reusable ice pack by mixing one part rubbing alcohol and two parts water in a sealable plastic bag, and freeze. Because it doesn't freeze solid, it's particularly handy to have for sore knees or elbows. It may help the pain to know you're saving at least $5 every time you pull it out of the freezer!

Use food for sore spots. Try putting a bag of frozen peas on an aching shoulder, or freeze a small ketchup packet from a fast-food restaurant to tuck onto a small, hard-to-reach sore spot. You have them in your house already—why not use them to save on ice packs from the pharmacy?

Insurance (car)

Buy in bulk. Buy your car and home insurance from the same company. Not only can you save up to 15 percent on separate car and home insurance costs, your

Take a class.

A defensive driving class, that is. You can get a 10 percent discount or more on your car insurance, and you'll learn how to stay away from trouble on the road, which may save you even more money in the long run. Ask your insurance provider or your state DMV for information on these classes.

insurance company will be less likely to drop you if you have an accident—it will want to keep the rest of your business.

Hit the delete button. Make sure you're not paying double for the same insurance. Read your policies carefully to determine if you're paying for life insurance (which you already have) as part of your car insurance. Dump any double coverage that you find.

Make your occupation work for you, even if you're retired. Ask your insurance company if it offers discounts for particular occupations. Some offer dollars off for teachers, engineers, and so on. See if your job, even your former job, has a payoff for you!

Update to keep costs down. Keep your insurance agent up to speed on changes that might affect your rates. Have you given up an extra car? Are you putting far less mileage on your car because of a new job or retirement? Only using it for "pleasure" driving, never for business? Even little changes can save you money, so be sure to make that call each year.

Ask for any and all discounts. Your insurance company or agent may not volunteer information about the many discounts available, so ask about discounts specifically: for car security systems, low mileage, a good driving record, safety features on your car, an older car, and more.

Keep quiet. Don't file small claims. If you do, your insurance company is more likely to raise your rates. Absorb the cost of scratches in the paint, dings in the body, or a cracked windscreen (if you don't have specific replacement coverage) to keep your rates from going up, up, up—or your policy being canceled altogether.

Invitations

Don't supersize. Choose regular-size invitations when you're planning a party. Oversize invitations will require additional postage (and will probably cost more, too).

Go high-tech. Send e-mail invitations to your next party. Emily Post may not agree, but you'll save on the cost of postage and the cost of the invitations—and possibly even on the gas used going to the post office!

Keep it on hand!

15 easy recipes for the most-used supplies in your home

Sure, we understand. Using brand-name products can be both convenient and reassuring. But if you want to bypass all the extra chemicals and packaging, it's oh-so-easy to make everyday household supplies at home. We've asked the experts for their best recipes for 15 items every household needs—including cleaners, bug repellents, even toothpaste! The results not only work spectacularly well but are easy to make, and, in some cases, will save you a small fortune!

YOUR COMPLETE HOUSE-CLEANING ARSENAL

✔ Tough Multi-Purpose Cleaner

When it comes to cleaning nonwood surfaces around your home, this cleaner is tough to beat—you might even say that it's "fantastic."

- 1 ½ pints water
- ⅓ cup rubbing alcohol
- 1 teaspoon clear household ammonia
- 1 teaspoon mild dishwashing liquid
- ½ teaspoon lemon juice
- 1 clean 32-ounce spray bottle

1. Combine the ingredients in the spray bottle and shake well before each use.

2. Spray on countertops, kitchen appliances and fixtures, and tile or painted surfaces.

3. Wipe down with a clean cloth or damp sponge.

✔ Super Window and Glass Cleaner

Made of ingredients you already have at home, the alcohol in this formula will keep glass from streaking.

- 3 ½ cups water
- ⅓ cup white vinegar
- ¼ cup rubbing alcohol
- 1 clean, 32-ounce spray bottle

1. Mix all the ingredients in the spray bottle. Shake well before using.

2. Spray on dirty windowpane or other glass surface.

3. Dry with crumpled newspaper.

✔ Dishwashing Liquid

This dishwashing soap for washing dishes by hand, unlike some of its commercial counterparts, is mild on your hands, too. Since soap flakes are not widely available, as they once were, it's usually necessary to make your own by grating a soap bar; it takes only a minute or so.

¼	cup soap flakes
1 ½	cups hot water
¼	cup glycerin
½	teaspoon lemon oil
1	clean, 16-ounce squirt bottle

1. To make the soap flakes, lightly grate a bar of pure soap, such as Ivory, on a coarse kitchen grater.

2. In a medium pitcher, pour the soap flakes into the hot water and stir with a fork until most of the soap has dissolved. Let the solution cool for 5 minutes.

3. Stir in the glycerin and lemon oil. A loose gel will form as it cools. Use the fork to break up any congealed parts and pour the liquid into the squirt bottle. Use 2 to 3 teaspoons per sink or dishpan of hot water to clean the dishes.

✔ Laundry Soap

This basic laundry soap gets clothes as clean as those fancy single-name commercial cleaners—it just costs a lot less!

½	cup soap flakes
½	cup baking soda
¼	cup washing soda
¼	cup borax
1	clean, 16-ounce plastic container with lid

1. To make the soap flakes, lightly grate a bar of pure soap, such as Ivory, on a coarse kitchen grater.

Soap flakes? Washing soda?

Once upon a time, the only cleaning ingredients you could buy at a store were the basic items used in our recipes—things like ammonia, baking soda, or vinegar. Today, many of the cleaning staples of yesteryear are hard to find. For example, soap flakes. Some stores still carry them, but one of the most popular brands—Ivory—stopped making them in the 1990s. As the recipes note, you can easily make soap flakes at home with a bar of soap and a kitchen grater.

Washing soda has also fallen off most stores' shelves. Washing soda is sodium carbonate—very similar to baking soda (sodium bicarbonate), but far more alkaline: it has a pH of 11, compared with 8.1 for baking soda and 7 for water, which is completely neutral. If you can't find washing soda, you can substitute baking soda, but it won't be as powerful of a cleaner. If you do find washing soda (often near the bleach or fabric softeners), use it carefully, wearing gloves. It's strong stuff. Added to a cleaning mix, it does a great job!

Finally, pine oil is an oil extracted from pine cones and trees. Once a popular cleaning ingredient and great for wood floors, it, too, is harder to find today but available at some grocery and hardware stores.

2. In a large bowl, mix all the ingredients together. Store in a tightly sealed plastic container.

3. Use about ½ cup of the mixture instead of detergent in each load of laundry.

✔ **Multi-Purpose Bathroom Disinfectant**

Here's a good, all-purpose disinfectant that is as easy to use and as effective as any commercial bathroom cleaner but is much less expensive.

2 teaspoons borax
½ teaspoon washing soda
2 tablespoons lemon juice
4 tablespoons white vinegar
3 cups very hot water
1 clean, 24-ounce spray bottle

1. Combine the borax, washing soda, lemon juice, and vinegar in the spray bottle.

2. Slowly add the hot water, then vigorously shake the bottle until the powdered ingredients have dissolved. Shake the bottle before each use.

3. Spray on tile and ceramic surfaces and wipe with a damp, clean cloth.

✔ **Pine Floor Cleaner**

You shouldn't have to spend a small fortune to give your no-wax floors a pine-fresh smell. This excellent cleaner will do the job for just a few cents per use!

½ cup soap flakes
¼ cup washing soda
1 cup salt
2 cups water
2 teaspoons pine oil
1 clean, 16-ounce plastic bottle with a tight-fitting lid
1 cup white vinegar

1. To make the soap flakes, lightly grate a bar of pure soap, such as Ivory, on a coarse kitchen grater.

2. In a saucepan over low heat, combine the soap, washing soda, salt, and water and stir until the soap, soda, and salt have dissolved.

3. Remove from the heat and allow the mixture to cool until it is lukewarm. Add the pine oil. Stir well, pour into the plastic bottle, and secure the top.

4. To use, pour 2 or 3 tablespoons of the cleaner into a half-bucket of water, stirring well. For large areas, you may need to double the amount.

5. After cleaning, add the vinegar to a half-bucket of clean water and rinse the floor.

IN YOUR GARDEN

✔ **Homemade Insecticide**

When aphids, whiteflies, and other insect pests become a problem in the garden or on your houseplants, make your own repellent from these kitchen-tested ingredients. (Don't forget to store it in a capped and labeled bottle in a child-proof cabinet.)

10 garlic cloves
1 tablespoon vegetable or mineral oil
3 cups hot water
1 teaspoon dishwashing soap (not laundry or dishwasher detergent)
1 clean 32-ounce spray bottle

1. In a blender, puree the garlic (skin and all) and oil.

2. Strain mixture through a sieve into a quart jar. Add water and dishwashing soap. Cap the jar and shake gently to mix. Decant the mixture into the spray bottle.

3. Spray infested plants, making sure to cover both sides of the leaves. Apply every 3 days for a week to control hatching insect eggs. Repeat as needed after rains or when problems arise.

✔ Stink 'Um Deer Spray

Deer have sensitive noses and are repelled by animal odors, especially that of spoiled eggs. Whip up this stinky brew, and deer will soon be feeding elsewhere.

- 1 egg
- 1 cup water
- ¼ cup garlic juice
- 1 tablespoon liquid dish detergent
- Scrap of panty hose
- Rubber band

1. In a blender, mix the egg, water, and garlic juice. Stir in detergent to avoid foaming. Pour solution into an open container and set in an out-of-nose range spot outdoors to age for 3 days.

2. Cover the siphon of a spray bottle with a scrap of panty hose held on with a rubber band to prevent clogging. Fill spray bottle with Stink 'Um and spray vulnerable plants. Repeat applications after rains.

✔ Spot Weed Killer

Weeds that pop up between flagstones and in cracks of the sidewalk are hard to dig out of the small crevices. Kill weeds in your terrace or walkway by dousing them with this simple laundry-room solution.

- Household bleach
- Boiling water

1. Prepare a solution of 5 percent bleach and 95 percent boiling water.

2. Douse weeds with the solution, wait a day, and check for withering. If the weeds resist, increase the percentage of bleach and repeat.

ESSENTIAL MEDICINE-CABINET SUPPLIES

✔ Healing Ointment for Cuts and Scrapes

You can have this ointment on hand to treat everyday cuts and scrapes as they arise, just as you would a tube of pricey commercial antiseptic.

- 1–1½ ounces cosmetic-grade beeswax, grated
- 1 cup olive oil or almond oil
- 2 capsules vitamin E, 400 IU
- 30 drops tea tree essential oil

20 drops spike lavender or
French lavender essential oil

10 drops chamomile
essential oil

10 drops fir essential oil

1. In the top of a double boiler over low heat, melt the beeswax. Stir in the olive or almond oil. Remove from the heat. Pierce each vitamin E capsule with a needle and squeeze the contents into the mixture. Then stir in the essential oils.

2. Pour into a small sterilized jar with a tight-fitting lid and store in a cool, dark place. Use as needed. Should last a year.

✔ **Green Aloe Moisturizing Lotion**

Cook up this delightful body lotion that has aloe vera, an antioxidant, as its primary ingredient.

1 cup aloe vera gel

1 teaspoon vitamin E oil (if necessary, break several capsules)

5–10 drops essential oil of your choosing

¾ ounce cosmetic-grade beeswax, grated or shaved

½ cup vegetable oil

1. In a medium bowl, stir together the aloe vera gel, vitamin E, and essential oil. Set aside.

> **Hiccup relief!**
>
> You can't find a remedy for hiccups in the drugstore, but you can easily make one yourself! But it takes courage. . . .
>
> The way to rid hiccups, say our experts? Put 2 to 3 teaspoons of sugar or a dry drink mix like lemonade crystals or hot chocolate in your mouth and try to swallow it all. Getting it down will take some effort—and that will short-circuit the hiccups!

2. In the top of a double boiler over simmering water, melt together the beeswax and vegetable oil. Stir until smooth and well blended. Remove from heat.

3. Slowly and continuously pour the melted mixture into the bowl with the aloe vera mixture, using a handheld electric mixer at slow speed to combine. Run a clean rubber spatula around the rim of the bowl to incorporate all the ingredients. Continue mixing until all the ingredients are blended.

4. Pour the final mixture into one sterilized 13-ounce jar or two sterilized 6-ounce jars with tight-fitting lids. You can use the sterilized canning jars, if you have them. Keep the lotion in the refrigerator for up to 6 weeks.

✔ Toothpaste

The tea tree oil gives this paste an additional antiseptic boost that will help prevent gum disease.

3 tablespoons baking soda
Water
10 drops tea tree essential oil
10 drops peppermint essential oil

1. In a small bowl, mix the baking soda with just enough water to make a paste. Add the tea tree and peppermint essential oils.

2. Use paste to brush your teeth and tongue. Cover the remaining paste and use for the next couple of days.

✔ Spicy, Minty Mouthwash

This simple recipe offers a kick that will make your mouth feel wonderful for hours, and doesn't burn your mouth as alcohol-laden commercial mouthwashes do.

1 cup water
1 teaspoon whole cloves
1 teaspoon ground cinnamon
1 teaspoon peppermint extract
2 teaspoons parsley

1. In a small saucepan, bring the water to a boil over medium heat. Remove the pan from the stove and stir in the cloves, cinnamon, peppermint extract, and parsley. Let mixture sit for 10 minutes. Strain off the solids.

2. Pour the liquid into a clean, tightly sealed container and store in the refrigerator, where it will keep indefinitely. Use as a gargle and mouthwash.

✔ Electrolyte Drink for Diarrhea

Diarrhea can drain your body of liquids and electrolytes quite quickly and dangerously. This easy, inexpensive juice drink helps maintain your body's equilibrium. (If your diarrhea persists for more than 24 hours, see a doctor.)

1 cup apple juice
2 cups water
½–1 teaspoon salt
Juice from a lemon or a lime

1. In a pitcher, combine the apple juice, water, salt, and lemon or lime juice. Store in the refrigerator.

2. Drink throughout the day to maintain hydration and proper balance of electrolytes.

Jeans

Flip over your jeans. To make jeans last longer, turn them inside out when you wash them (in cold water on the gentle cycle). If some of the dye escapes from the fabric during the wash, it has a better chance of being reabsorbed into the legs.

Patch 'em up. Are your favorite jeans soft and comfortable and beautifully worn—and in danger of ripping? If so, reinforce the insides of the knees, the corners of pockets, and any other places that look likely to split with iron-on patches. You'll help make your beloved jeans last even longer.

Wash and dry with care. Don't toss your jeans into the wash if you've worn them only once. Wait until they're dirty enough to need cleaning. And don't just throw them in the dryer, either. Use a no-heat setting, or better yet, hang them to dry, out of direct sunlight. You'll save wear and tear on your jeans and on your energy bill, too.

Jewelry

Fix it and forget it. Reset loose stones in your costume jewelry easily and inexpensively with nail polish. Simply use clear nail polish as the glue; it's a quick fix that no one will detect.

Jewelry box

Do double duty. Why spend money on a fancy jewelry box when any number of other organizers will serve the same purpose just as well or even better? Try using an ice-cube tray, a silverware tray, or a craft box designed for beads if you want to separate your jewelry. Hang your necklaces and bracelets from push-pins on a bulletin board. Put post earrings on a mesh pen holder or an upended colander. Your choices are unlimited (and the price is right!).

Jigsaw puzzle

A custom-made puzzle for the price of cardboard.

Make a jigsaw puzzle by gluing leftover wallpaper or magazine photos, or even a picture you took yourself, enlarged on the computer, onto cardboard. When it dries, cut it up into the kinds of pieces—small or large, simple or complex—that you want for your puzzle. You'll save $10 to $20 just by using what you have on hand, and any kids in the family will be thrilled.

Keys

Lock out the locksmith. Make an extra set of house and car keys and give them to a trusted neighbor or friend. Next time you lose your keys or lock them in the house or car, you'll save yourself the expense of a locksmith.

Kitty litter

Make it cheap and easy. There's no need to spend a fortune on kitty litter. Just mix a 75-cent box of baking soda with an inexpensive brand of cat litter for immediate savings and the same odor effectiveness of the more expensive brands.

Keep it in your car.

Strange as it sounds, you should keep kitty litter in your trunk during the winter months. It provides excellent traction if you get stuck and is a lot cheaper than a tow truck.

Knee pads

Dig up your garden, not your pants. Save wear and tear on your pants when you garden by wrapping a plastic bag around each knee. You'll want to spend your money on beautiful flowers, not on a new pair of pants.

A mouse for inside and out. Use old computer mouse pads when you need to kneel in the garden. They'll cushion your knees just as well as cushions you buy at your garden store.

Laundry

A little care goes a long way. Turn dark-colored clothing inside out in the wash to prolong the color. Put lingerie and other fine washables in mesh bags to prevent snagging.

Keep it cold. Do your wash (including the rinse cycle) in cold water. A typical family of four can save $120 per year by not using hot water in the washing machine.

Give it a soak. Stained white tablecloths and napkins aren't destined for the dumpster or pricey store-bought solutions. Instead, soak them in a solution of water and 2 tablespoons of baking soda for three hours or overnight, then launder as usual.

Lawn

Step on it. Don't waste water (and money) on your lawn; an average lawn requires just one hour of watering per week. How can you tell if yours is dry? Step on the grass. If the blades don't jump back up, you need to water. If they spring back, hold off on the sprinklers.

Offer an early drink. Water your plants and your lawn early in the morning. If you water later, the sun will burn off the moisture you so carefully put down before it has a chance to soak in.

Lawn mower

Leave it long. If you cut your grass too short, you'll cut down on saving water (and money). Set your mower blades to the 3-inch setting. Taller grass holds water longer than shorter grass.

Keep it "reel." If you have a small lawn, buy an old-fashioned push lawn mower—also known as a reel mower—rather than a fuel-powered mower. You'll easily save at least $100 on the transaction, you won't have to pay for gas or tune-ups, and you'll get great exercise every time you mow the lawn.

Lighting

A bright idea. Install motion-detector lights or timers on outdoor lights that may inadvertently get left on during the day. The automatic shut-off will give you peace of mind—and a few extra dollars.

Convert to CFLs. Use compact fluorescent light (CFL) bulbs. They last 8 to 10 times longer than incandescent bulbs, put out less heat than incandescents, and, most importantly, use minimal energy. Putting CFLs in just a quarter of your fixtures may cut your lighting bill in half. Put them in all your fixtures, and watch the savings skyrocket!

Three ways to save. If you haven't yet converted to CFLs, use three-way bulbs in your light fixtures. Use the lowest wattage whenever possible, and you'll save on electricity costs.

Stick to the task. Rather than light an entire room when you're working in one corner, use efficient task lighting. It's an easy way to pay for only what you use.

Lotion

Stand your lotion on its head. Turn your almost-empty moisturizer bottle upside down. The lotion will fall into the cap, and you'll squeeze several more uses out of the bottle. (You can do the same with shampoo and conditioner and any other cosmetic that will stand upside down.)

Magazines

Get your fix with a friend. Are you hooked on magazines but discovering that you have an expensive habit? Ask a few like-minded friends to each subscribe to one magazine, then swap the magazines so everyone gets to read them all. Depending on the number of magazines (and friends) involved, you could save a bundle.

Makeup

Cap your costs. Don't bother buying concealer if you already use foundation. You can find the perfect cover-up in the cap, where the foundation has settled. It's the right consistency, and you can't find a better color match!

Use it in a different form. If your lipstick is broken, don't give up on it. Instead, push the remainder of the lipstick down into the tube, and then use a lip brush to apply it. You can also put the broken bullet into a small empty makeup container, melt it with a blow-dryer, let it dry, then use it in its new form.

Take it off—take it all off. Try some moisturizer in place of your expensive makeup remover. It's a perfect substitute: It removes makeup quickly and easily for a lot less, and you don't have to buy extra products.

continued on page 114

Money—the big financial questions

No matter what the market does, you should know how to shore up your resources so you won't have to worry about every little hiccup. Here are time-tested strategies you can master—how to spend less, reduce your debt, make the most of your tax breaks, invest wisely, and finance your retirement. The idea, says William Speciale, a Boston-based advisor with the financial planning firm Daintree Advisors, is to focus on what you can control: "Little steps can really make a huge difference."

TAXES

✔ **Forget the short form.**
Most taxpayers—65 percent of us, to be specific—just take the standard deduction. But you may save money by itemizing your deductible expenses. It doesn't matter if you use an online program, a current tax guide, or a storefront preparer. Out-of-pocket health-care charges, business expenses (including some for job searches), and charitable donations are just a few of the items you may be able to deduct. Fill out the long form, known as the 1040, and compare numbers. If your total deductions are greater than the standard deduction, you'll save money by itemizing when you file.

✔ **Your employed kids should file a tax return.**
The IRS doesn't care how old they are. If they earn more than $5,450 in a given year (in wages and/or interest income), they have to file—even if you claim them as dependents. And if they make less than that, they should still file because they'll get back all the money their employer withheld. Help them fill out the paperwork. It's a great learning experience that may earn them some extra cash.

✔ **Avoid a tax refund.**
You may feel giddy knowing you'll get a check from the IRS this spring, but you shouldn't. Getting money back means you're essentially lending money,

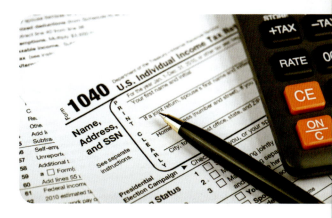

interest free, to the government for the year. Better to have that cash in your account than lend it to Uncle Sam. So if you've been getting big refunds or have had a big life change (a marriage, a baby, a divorce, a radical increase or decrease in income), adjust the withholding allowances on your W-4 form. You can do that at irs.gov. Use the withholding calculator to determine the correct figure for you. Then print a new W-4, fill it out, and give it to your payroll department.

✔ **Avoid "rapid refund" programs.**
Sure, they sound great. After all, what can be better than getting your money fast? A tax-prep chain might try to get you to agree to one of these "instant" or "anticipation" options. Don't take the bait. This is not your refund. It's a loan—and a very high-interest loan at that. Some rates can be 120 percent or more. If you file electronically, even if it's through a tax chain, the IRS will deposit your refund directly into your bank account within a week or two.

CHECKING AND SAVINGS

✔ **Make sure your free checking is really free.**
A lot of banks advertise it, but read the fine print. If the minimum balance is steep— thousands of dollars, in some cases—look for a bank with no minimum requirement. This could save $100 a year or more. Bankrate.com is a good site for comparing accounts. (And don't waste $2 on ATM withdrawals at another bank's machines.)

✔ **Bank online.**
You'll be surprised how easy it is to pay bills, transfer funds, save

automatically, and keep track of it all. In fact, gathering records at tax time will be a cinch. And by setting up the automatic bill-payment option, you'll help protect your credit score. Banking online is actually safer than banking at a brick-and-mortar institution. Banks have spent a fortune to make sure their sites are among the most secure on the Internet.

✔ Keep your money in super-safe places.

Aim to amass at least six months of emergency expenses, in case you lose your job or become disabled. Where's the best place to keep it? FDIC-insured bank savings, CDs, and money-market accounts are still three of the most secure places. Money-market funds that invest in Treasury bills are super-safe, too, but low yielding. Internet banks and credit unions tend to pay higher interest rates, but go to fdic.gov and check to make sure they offer the same government-insured guarantee. Look into Series I bonds, or I bonds, which are just as safe and are guaranteed to

keep up with inflation. They're also free from state and local taxes (and possibly federal tax, if you use them for college costs). The downside? You can't redeem them for at least a year. And if you cash them in before five years, there's a small penalty. Other savings options, including corporate and tax-exempt money-market funds, are a bit riskier. Compare yields at cranedata.us.

DEBT

✔ Cut up your extra credit cards.

But don't close the accounts. Yes, it's smart to reduce your temptation to splurge by destroying your cards. But if you actually cancel them, it could hurt your credit rating. Here's why: Lenders worry about how close you are to using all the credit available to you. If you close an account, you lose its credit

line. As a result, you are using a greater portion of the reduced amount you can now borrow. How many cards do you need? While the average American household has nine, two or three active cards should be plenty.

✔ Pay your bills on time.

A single late payment means that you could pay a much higher interest rate on any future loans and on your existing credit card accounts. That's because even one missed payment can lower your credit score by as much as 100 points. That plunge means that lenders view you as a risky customer. If you're shopping around for a mortgage, you could end up paying as much as a full percentage point more. That's an increase that could ultimately cost you tens of thousands of dollars in interest. Set up automatic payments to make sure you're never late on your major bills. The sooner you can show lenders you're back on track, the better.

✔ Pay $10 more each month.

Most American households keep their credit balances at around $2,000, but about 10 to 15 percent carry balances that are $9,000 or higher. If you paid the minimum $224 required on that $9,000 balance each month, it would take you 31 years and more than $13,000 in interest to pay it off. Increasing your payment by just $10 a month, to $234, until you've paid off the balance would save you $8,900. And you'd get rid of the debt in five years. (To check how long it will take you to pay off your own balances, try the debt pay down calculator at bankrate.com.)

✔ Put your savings to work.

Many people who are deep in debt usually have some savings stashed in a bank account. They argue that they don't want to use their hard-earned savings to pay off debt. But do the math: It would make sense to keep the money in savings only if the bank is paying you an interest rate higher than the one your credit cards charge. Paying off a card with an interest rate of 13 percent is the equivalent of earning 13 percent interest on your money after taxes. There are no savings or investment options with that kind of guarantee. Experts caution that you still want to keep emergency cash on hand. A good rule is to take 5 percent of your paycheck to pay off debt and put an additional 5 percent into savings.

✔ **Pay more on your mortgage.**
You may have heard that because the interest is tax deductible, a mortgage is a good debt. But even if you're getting a tax break, you're still paying interest—and the longer you've had the mortgage, the smaller the tax break (because you pay less interest each year). As with all debt, paying it off sooner is better. So once you've paid off your credit cards and other high-rate debt, go ahead and add an extra payment each year (or spread it out over 12 months). If you do that over the life of a 30-year fixed loan with a rate of 6 percent, you'll shave roughly 20 percent off the total interest you pay. On a $150,000 mortgage, that means saving about $26,000.

✔ **Reduce your credit card interest rate.**
It may be time to get nervy with the credit card companies. If you pay your bill on time and your credit card company still raises your rates or lowers your limits, call the company's toll-free number (ask for the retention department) and explain that you're thinking of taking your business elsewhere. You may reap a rate reduction. And credit crunch or not, banks are still motivated to keep good customers. And check your accounts often. These days, banks are increasing rates even on good customers.

✔ **Get your credit report for free.**
You're entitled to one free report from each of the three credit bureaus (Experian, TransUnion, and Equifax) every year. Beware, though. Many sites advertising "free credit reports" are actually fronts for companies trying to sell you services—credit monitoring, debt consolidation, credit repair—most of which you don't need. The reports are free, but you'll be automatically signed up and billed for these products. Get your reports from AnnualCreditReport. com, which is sponsored by the three bureaus and the Federal Trade Commission. You can

purchase extras on this site, too, but just stick with the free reports. If you want to see your credit scores (a numerical representation of how good a credit risk you are), you'll have to pay $59.85 at myfico.com.

INSURANCE

✔ Shop around for car insurance.

An online search and a few phone calls can turn up vastly different rates in the same area. You'll also want to ask about lesser-known breaks. For example, even if your kids are grown and out of the house, they might be able to get a substantial discount if they insure their cars through the company you use.

✔ Sign up for an FSA.

Many employers offer flexible spending accounts (FSAs) as a way to set aside part of your salary for health-care and child-care costs. You can pay for everything from Band-Aids to orthodontic work with pretax money, which translates into a discount of about 30 percent or more, depending on your tax bracket. But plan carefully. If you don't use all the money in your account within the year (at many companies, you have until March 15 of the following year to submit receipts), you lose whatever's left.

✔ Keep grown kids on your health insurance policy.

If you're going to end up lending (or giving) your children money for coverage, it's much cheaper to keep them on your policy as long as possible. Under the Affordable Care Act, you can do this until they are 26, whether they're still in school or not. (New Jersey will give you until they turn 30.) Check out the latest information at HealthCare.gov.

✔ **Hold off on that long-term-care insurance.**

The soaring cost of extended nursing care has prompted many people in their forties and fifties to sign up for long-term-care insurance in order to lock in a rate. It's true that the premiums go up as you get older, but not by the huge amount you might expect. According to data collected by America's Health Insurance Plans, a 65-year-old may end up paying just $126 more a year than someone who bought a policy at age 55. During those ten years, that person would spend close to $19,000 on coverage, even though he or she probably won't need it until age 83 or so (if at all). Depending on your health, the best time to buy is between 60 and 65. Until then, make retirement savings the priority, not long-term-care insurance.

✔ **Up for disability insurance.**
It helps protect your income in the event you become unable to work for a long period. Ideally, you should have enough to replace 60 to 70 percent of your salary. If your company plan doesn't provide this much coverage, consider buying more on your own. It can be costly, but it's worth it. Visit AffordableInsuranceProtection. com or unum.com for quotes.

✔ **Think twice about life insurance.**
If you don't have dependents, you may not need it. If you do have kids or other dependents, you're probably better off with term life insurance until, say, your children are grown and can take care of themselves. It's generally less expensive than whole-life or other types of policies that build up value until you die or cash them in. Agents will tell you that whole-life insurance is a good investment because your money builds up tax-free, but these policies often have very high fees. You're better off putting that money toward your 401(k) and IRA instead. To comparison shop for term life policies, try term4sale.com.

✔ **Write your will.**
Although no one likes to think about dying, you need to. A will doesn't have to be a fancy contract

that teams of lawyers slave over. It's just a written record of whom you want to entrust your kids and assets to when you die. You can write one using a simple boilerplate form and then sign it in the presence of witnesses (usually two people who aren't named in the will). You'll also want to make sure all the beneficiaries on your life insurance policies and bank and retirement accounts are up-to-date.

INVESTMENTS

✔ **Stay away from individual stocks.**

In spite of what you may hear from your cousin the broker, buying the stock of a single company is generally not wise. It's essentially putting all your eggs in one basket—and paying broker fees that could eat up your earnings. In fact, you don't really need a broker. Instead of buying individual stocks, invest directly in mutual funds, which spread your dollars among a group of stocks. It's usually safer, cheaper, and simpler. But remember, you should do this only with money you can invest long term and can afford to lose in the short term.

✔ **Stick with index funds.**

You'll want to go with a special type of mutual fund called an index fund, which buys a little piece of each of the companies that make up established market benchmarks like the S&P 500. One of the best-kept secrets of investing is that in the long run, index funds perform at least as well as the funds that charge high fees and have a professional stock picker making the choices. For a list of low-cost index funds, go to vanguard.com or fidelity.com.

✔ Don't buy investment products from your bank.

Banks sell a wide range of mutual funds, annuities, and individual stocks and bonds. These aren't FDIC-insured, and they tend to be more expensive than what you could get elsewhere because banks usually charge high sales commissions. Buy directly from mutual fund companies instead. Go with companies like Vanguard or Fidelity, which charge low fees and no commissions.

✔ Build a portfolio.

The rule of thumb is to put 50 percent of your long-term savings in stocks and 30 percent in bonds and keep 20 percent available in cash (that means in a savings or money-market account where you can withdraw it at a moment's notice). In tough times especially, getting the right mix will depend on the risk you're willing to take and how soon you'll need your money. Stocks are generally more risky than bonds, but there are exceptions. For example, bonds issued by companies that are in questionable financial health—called junk bonds or, more euphemistically, high-yield bonds—are a lot riskier than, say, stock in utility companies.

RETIREMENT

✔ Contribute to your company's 401(k).

If your company matches funds, sign up. This will be the best investment you can possibly make. Typically, a company will kick in 50 cents for every dollar you save, up to 6 percent of your salary. That's the equivalent of earning an immediate 50 percent return—a rate you can't get anywhere. Yet incredibly, one in three American workers who are eligible isn't taking full advantage of it. With the matching funds, you can more than double the size of your 401(k) in 20 years, even if the stock market remains flat. For a family making $44,000, your contribution may cost you as little as $30 a week, money you won't even miss after a while.

✔ Put retirement savings ahead of college savings.

This sounds crazy to parents who need to come up with tuition money well before it's time to retire. But because of the tax breaks and the flexibility of retirement accounts, you're much better off contributing to a 401(k) or an IRA and taking out loans for college. Many people don't realize that the contributions you put in Roth IRAs can be withdrawn free of penalties at any time. That's very different from the college savings plans, called 529s, that smack you with a significant penalty if the money is not used for college. Another plus: Most schools don't count money in your retirement accounts when assessing how much financial aid they'll offer you.

✔ **Say no to company stock.**
Think of Lehman Brothers, Bear Stearns, and Enron. All were once on top, but when they went under, many employees were left without jobs and with retirement accounts that were overloaded with worthless company stock. You already have a huge stake in the company because you depend on it for your paycheck.

Don't risk your retirement money as well. If your employer offers company stock as a 401(k) option, don't take it. If you get company stock as part of your matching-funds plan, sell it as soon as you're allowed to, and switch that money into some other type of investment. Ask your HR representative for details.

✔ **Don't worry about Social Security.**
You've probably heard the dire predictions that anyone younger than 35 can't expect to collect Social Security. Even in bleak economic scenarios, though, Social Security will probably pay you 65 to 80 percent of your currently promised benefits. And with some fairly modest changes—like raising the retirement age or increasing payroll taxes for anyone earning more than $250,000 annually—the system can be shored up for decades to come. Make sure you're saving enough so you don't have to count on the program for your entire retirement income.

continued from page 103

Matches

Don't eat the match. Why spend money on extra-long matches when you probably have a perfectly good substitute on hand? Use a piece of uncooked spaghetti next time you need to light a hard-to-reach wick or multiple candles.

Meat

Tough it out. You know that tougher meats are less expensive than tender meats. But did you know that many butchers will run these cheaper cuts through the tenderizer if you ask? Your tough cut will turn into a more tender bite at no cost.

A wise buy for a wise guy (or gal). Boneless meat may cost more per pound, but it usually gives you more for your money than a cut filled with fat and bone.

Slice it thin to keep your wallet fat.

Ask your deli man or woman to slice your meat and cheese thinner than usual. You'll most likely use less in each sandwich you make, which is good for your wallet and your waistline.

Microwave

Zap it once to save twice. According to the U.S. Department of Energy and the Environmental Protection Agency, using your microwave oven for small portions can reduce your cooking energy by up to 80 percent. Plus, your air-conditioning costs will be lower in the summer if you use your microwave, since it doesn't generate heat the way your stove or oven does.

Mop pads

Flip it. After you've used your disposable mop pad, turn it over and use the other side. Then throw it away, knowing you've gotten twice your money's worth.

Movies

The early bird gets the . . . movie. Want to see a first-run movie for less than the cost of a child's ticket? Many theaters offer discounts on the first matinee showing of the day, when the seats might otherwise be unoccupied.

Movie magic for members. Costco members can buy movie tickets at discounted rates for theater chains including AMC, Cinemark, and Regal Entertainment. You buy in bulk (five tickets at a time) and save about $2 per ticket.

Mulch

Chips all around. Rather than buying expensive garden mulch, contact your local tree doctor or sawmill, and ask them to deliver wood chips directly to your backyard. Biodegradeable, safe, and natural looking, this terrific mulch also may be free or much less expensive than buying bags of mulch.

Museums

Free art. Most private museums, both large and small, offer free admission on certain days or at certain times. And independent art gallery openings are usually free and open to the public. Plus you may score a free glass of wine, a cube of cheese, and a chance to talk to the artist.

Turn it off and save.
Don't wait until your dish is completely cooked. Turn off the oven a few minutes before the recipe says you should. The heat left in the oven is sufficient for finishing the meal.

Nails

Fingernails, that is. Stretch out the time between nail appointments: if you normally get your nails done once a week, mark your calendar to get them done once every two weeks instead. At $10 an appointment, you'll save $260 per year, not including tips! Ask the manicurist not to put a sealing topcoat on your nails. The thicker the coating, the faster it will peel off.

Very cool nails! Cold nail polish lasts longer and can be applied more smoothly. So take it out of the closet or medicine cabinet (or wherever you store it) and put it in the refrigerator.

Get more from your manicure. Your manicure will last longer if you clean your nails with vinegar. Use a cotton ball to apply the vinegar before you paint your nails, then enjoy the extra time you have before your next manicure.

Napkins

Cut from the right cloth. Sometimes it's hard to remember that cloth napkins still exist. They may require a little care, but they'll add a touch of elegance to your table— and more importantly, save you money over paper napkins in the long run.

National parks

Spend $10 to save hundreds. Over 61? If you enjoy national parks, you'll enjoy the savings you can get with the America the Beautiful Senior Pass. As long as you're a citizen or permanent resident of the United

States and at least 62 years old, you can buy this pass for $10 and get free or reduced admission to any federal recreation site—for the rest of your life! Get the pass from a national park, wildlife refuge, or participating federal recreation site or office.

Newspapers

Let's make a deal. Call your local newspaper and ask if it offers a discount for paying for your subscription a year in advance.

Pick and choose for less. Do you read only a few sections of the mammoth Sunday newspaper? If so, ask friends who always get the Sunday paper to give you the sections you like when they're done with them. You'll avoid waste—and the cost of the Sunday paper.

Save $4 on Sunday. If you're a news fiend, save money by swapping different Sunday newspapers with a friend. You read one in the morning, he reads the other, then you swap around noon. Or if you read only one Sunday newspaper, save several dollars by taking turns buying it. Just be sure to set a time to turn over the newspaper to your friend (and vice versa).

Dispense with the subscription altogether. Nearly all the major national newspapers in the United States can now be read online for free, although many limit the number of free articles you can read per month. You

continued on page 123

Never buy it again!
Grocery store items best made at home

With the rising costs of groceries, we'd all love to save a few bucks at the checkout line. Now you can easily slash your bill with some clever shopping moves and DIY recipes. Manufacturers would like to make you think you're getting a good deal in exchange for convenience, but it's really just eating away at your food budget. Don't be fooled any longer. Cross these items off your list for good!

1. "GOURMET" FROZEN VEGETABLES.

Sure, you can buy an 8-ounce packet of peas in an herbed butter sauce, but why do so when you can make your own? Just cook the peas, add a pat of butter and sprinkle on some herbs that you already have on hand. The same thing goes for carrots with dill sauce and other gourmet veggies.

2. MICROWAVE SANDWICHES.

When you buy a premade sandwich, you're really just paying for its elaborate packaging—plus a whole lot of salt, fat, and unnecessary additives. For the average cost of one of these babies ($2.50 to $3 per sandwich), you could make a bigger, better, and more nutritious version yourself.

3. PREMIUM FROZEN FRUIT BARS.

At nearly $2 per bar, frozen "all fruit" or "fruit and juice" bars may not be rich in calories, but they are certainly rich in price. Make your own at home—and get the flavors you want. The only equipment you need is a blender, a plastic reusable ice-pop mold (on sale at discount stores for about 99 cents each), or small paper cups and pop sticks or wooden skewers.

To make four pops, just throw 2 cups cut-up fruit, 1 tablespoon sugar, and 1 teaspoon lemon or lime juice into a blender. Cover and blend until smooth. You might wish to add 1 to 2 tablespoons of water so the final mix is a thick slush. Pour into 4-ounce pop molds or paper cups, insert sticks, and freeze until solid.

4. BOXED RICE "ENTREE" OR SIDE-DISH MIXES.

These consist basically of rice, salt, and spices— yet they're priced way beyond the ingredients sold individually. Yes, there are a few flavorings included, but they're probably ones you have in your pantry already. Buy a bag of rice, measure out what you need, add your own herbs and other seasonings, and cook the rice according to package directions.

5. ENERGY OR PROTEIN BARS.

These calorie-laden bars are usually stacked at the checkout counter because they depend on impulse buyers who grab them, thinking they are more wholesome than a candy bar. Unfortunately, they can have very high fat and sugar contents and are often as caloric as a regular candy bar. They're also two to three times more expensive than a candy bar at $2 to $3 a bar. If you need a boost, a vitamin-rich piece of fruit, a yogurt, or a small handful of nuts is more satiating and less expensive!

6. SPICE MIXES.

Spice mixes like grill seasoning and rib rubs might seem like a good buy because they contain a lot of spices that you would have to buy individually. Well, check the label; we predict the first ingredient you will see on the package is salt, followed by the vague "herbs and spices." Look in your own pantry, and you'll probably be surprised to discover just how many herbs you already have on hand. Many cookbooks today include spice mix recipes, particularly grilling cookbooks. But the great thing about spice mixes is that you can improvise as much as you want. Make your own custom combos and save a fortune.

7. POWDERED ICED TEA MIXES OR PREPARED FLAVORED ICED TEA.

Powdered and gourmet iced teas are really a rip-off! It's much cheaper to make your own iced tea from actual (inexpensive) tea bags and keep a jug in the fridge. Plus, many mixes and preparations are loaded with high-fructose corn syrup and other sugars, along with artificial flavors. So make your own, and get creative!

To make 32 ounces of iced tea, it usually takes 8 bags of black tea or 10 bags of herbal, green, or white tea. Most tea-bag boxes have recipes, so just follow along. If you like your tea sweet but want to keep calories down, skip the sugar and add fruit juice instead.

8. BOTTLED WATER.

Bottled water is a bad investment for so many reasons. It's expensive compared to what's coming out of the tap, its cost to the environment is high (it takes a lot of fossil fuel to produce and ship all those bottles), and it's not even better for your health than the stuff running down your drain! Even taking into account the cost of filters, water from home is still much cheaper than bottled water, which can run up to $1 to $3 a pop.

If you have well water and it really does not taste good (even with help from a filter), or if you are pregnant or have a baby at home and haven't had your well water tested recently, buy jugs of distilled or "nursery" water at big discount stores. They usually cost between 79 cents and 99 cents for 1 gallon (as opposed to $1.50 for 8 ounces of "designer" water). And you can reuse the jugs to store homemade iced tea, flavored waters, or, when their tops are cut off, all sorts of household odds and ends.

9. SALAD KITS.

Washed and bagged greens can be a time-saver, but they can cost three times as much as buying the same amount of a head of lettuce. Even more expensive are "salad kits," where you get some greens, a small bag of dressing, and a small bag of croutons. Skip these altogether. Make your own croutons by toasting cut-up stale bread you would otherwise toss,

Makin' gravy

We know many an accomplished cook who is completely intimidated by the thought of making old-fashioned gravy for their mashed potatoes or roast beef. So they turn to salty, chemical-filled canned gravy or gravy packets. Truth is, making gravy is easy. All you need is flour or cornstarch, butter or margarine, and stock. Then add mushrooms, herbs, spices, and more to give it a unique flavor.

Here's an easy recipe for you to follow that can be modified dozens of ways. Yield: About 2 cups. Time: About 10–15 minutes

EASY GRAVY

4   tablespoons unsalted butter or margarine

¼   cup all-purpose flour or cornstarch

¼   teaspoon salt (or to taste)

⅛   teaspoon freshly ground pepper (or to taste)

2   cups turkey, chicken, or beef broth (low-sodium if using packaged)

In a saucepan, melt the butter over medium heat, then add the flour, whisking until a smooth paste is formed. Add salt and pepper. Continue cooking until the mixture browns to a light toasty color (3–5 minutes). Turn the heat to low and slowly add broth, whisking constantly. Once the liquid is incorporated, turn the heat back to medium, and bring to a slow boil until thickened. Taste and adjust for seasoning, if necessary.

Modifications

Replace some of the liquid with dry, white wine for depth of flavor; sautéed mushrooms also add richness; dried oregano, basil, rosemary, or sage complement fowl or beef dishes; a tablespoon of sherry added at the end gives a sophisticated punch; likewise, a tablespoon of cream adds decadence and makes this truly a special sauce.

and try mixing your own salad dressing.

10. INDIVIDUAL SERVINGS OF ANYTHING.

The recent trend to package small quantities into 100-calorie snack packs is a way for food-makers to get more money from unsuspecting consumers. The price "per unit" cost of these items is significantly more than if you had just bought one big box of cheese crackers or bag of chips. This is exactly what you should do. Buy the big box and then parcel out single servings and store them in small, reusable storage bags.

11. TRAIL MIX.

We checked unit prices of those small bags of trail mix hanging in the candy aisle not that long ago and were shocked to find that they cost about $10 a pound! Make your own for much, much less with a 1-pound can of dry roasted peanuts, 1 cup of raisins, and a handful of almonds, dried fruit, and candy coated chocolate. The best part about making your own is that you only include the things you like! Keep the mixture in a plastic or glass container with a tight lid for up to 3 weeks.

12. "SNACK" OR "LUNCH" PACKS.

These "all-inclusive" food trays might seem reasonably priced (from $2.50 to $4.00), but you're actually paying for the highly designed label, wrapper, and specially molded tray. They only contain a few crackers and small pieces of cheese and lunch meat.

The actual edible ingredients are worth just pennies and are filled with salt.

13. GOURMET ICE CREAM.

It's painful to watch someone actually pay $6 for a gallon of designer-brand ice cream. Don't bother. There's usually at least one brand or other on sale, and you can easily dress up store brands with your own additives like chunky bits of chocolate or crushed cookie. If you do like the premium brands, wait for that three-week sales cycle to kick in and stock up when your favorite flavor is half price.

14. PREFORMED MEAT PATTIES.

Frozen burgers, beef or otherwise, are more expensive than buying the ground meat in bulk and making patties yourself. We timed it—it takes less than 10 seconds to form a flat circle and throw it on the grill! Also, there's some evidence that preformed meat patties might contain more E. coli than regular ground meat. In fact, most of the recent beef recalls have involved premade frozen beef patties. Fresh is definitely better!

continued from page 117

may have to register, which is also free, but in exchange you'll get news that's frequently updated, as well as additional photos, interactive graphics (at some sites), and, in many papers, additional articles and details there weren't room for in the printed paper.

Notary

A notary for nothing. Where can you get important documents notarized for free? Try your bank, the library, your employer, or a local government office. Call to make sure this service is offered (and that it's free) before you head out the door.

Obedience school

Sit, stay, save! Whether you enroll your dog in obedience school or train him yourself, you'll find savings in his good behavior. Because he'll be less likely to run into the street or eat things he shouldn't, you may save the price of medicine or even a big vet bill.

Odd jobs

Go the nonprofessional route. You don't always need an expensive professional to help you with jobs around the house. Call the job placement office at your local college to get students to help you with moving furniture, painting, gardening, lawn care, and more.

Orange juice

Cycling for sales. Start paying attention to when your grocery store puts your favorite brand of orange juice on sale. Chances are, you'll discover a pattern, or sales cycle. Soon you'll know when to buy orange juice and when not to. Sales cycles apply to ice cream, pasta, and cereal, too. When it's on sale, buy two or three and store them.

Outdoor furniture

Towel it off. Make your vinyl outdoor furniture last longer by sitting on a towel if you're wearing sunscreen. The sunscreen can eat away at the furniture's protective coating, allowing dirt to lodge permanently in the destroyed coating—making it impossible to clean. So sit on a towel and save yourself the cost of new furniture.

Oven

Keep it closed. Try not to open the oven door to check on the progress of your dish—the oven temperature drops by about 25 degrees every time you do (and you'll have to pay to get the heat back up to the right level). Use a good old-fashioned timer instead.

Choose your dish wisely. Use glass or ceramic baking dishes in your oven. Because glass conducts heat differently than metal, you can lower the temperature about 25 degrees (from the temperature the recipe says), and your food will still cook at the same rate.

Double your money. Save on energy bills by cooking two dishes in the oven at once. You can cook two items for the same meal—a chicken for dinner and brownies for dessert—or two items for two different meals, such as a roast for dinner and cinnamon rolls for breakfast the next day.

Over-the-counter medicines

Look past the packaging. Just as you save by buying generic prescription drugs, you can save by buying store brands of over-the-counter medications. Other than the packaging and, most importantly, the price, store brands are often no different from name-brand medications. Read the fine print to find the name and percentage of active ingredients—if they are the same as the active ingredients on the big-name brand, it's the same stuff. Ask the pharmacist if you have any doubts.

Price your pills. And your gel caps and your capsules. You may find that each form of your medicine carries a different price tag. Choose the right form—and the right price—for you.

Overdraft protection

Guard your checking account. Sign up for overdraft protection at your bank, just in case. It usually costs nothing and saves you the possible expense of returned-check fees.

Owner's manuals

Save instructions to save money. Keep all owner's manuals, receipts, and warranties. You may be able to easily fix your appliance, tool, or electronic device by consulting the manual, or you may be able to get it fixed for free if you check your warranty. If you've lost the manual, these days you can probably find it online—search for the brand name and the type of product.

Packing material

Ship and save. Don't waste your money on bubble wrap or other shipping materials. Just insert a straw into an almost-closed zip-top bag, and inflate the bag. Remove the straw, zip the bag tightly shut, and use as packing material.

Painting

Roll up the savings. Put a plastic grocery bag completely around your roller pan, roller inside, when you're in the midst of paint jobs around the house. If you tie the bag closed around the pan, the paint will stay fresh for up to several days. When you're done, simply wash the roller and throw away the bag (and the pan, if it's a disposable one). You'll save time on clean-up and money on multiple roller pans.

Pantry

Stay organized. You'll save two ways if you keep your pantry organized: you won't go to the grocery store as often because you'll know what you have (thereby avoiding impulse purchases), and you won't buy the same item that's already sitting on your pantry shelf.

Paper towels

Mop up the savings. Stop using paper towels every time you have a spill. Use a handy-dandy sponge and discover savings every time you keep a paper towel on the roll.

Place mats

Place a towel, not a mat. Use brightly colored dishtowels for slightly oversize place mats. They're less expensive than fabric place mats and easier to clean. If you buy the dishtowels in bulk, you can save even more.

Hit the fabric shop. Like to sew? Even if you don't, most fabric shops offer bits and remnants of great material in pieces too small to sell by the yard at ridiculously low costs. Pick up what appeals to you, and sew a straight hem around the edge. Presto! Instant place mats!

Plants

Look forward to an eternal spring. Plant bulbs and perennials, which bloom year after year, rather than annuals that you have to replace every spring.

Save on seeds. Collect seeds in the fall that you can plant in the spring. Put dry seeds from flowers like zinnias and cosmos in a paper bag, and store the bag until you're ready to plant the seeds the following year. You'll have beautiful flowers for free!

Go native. Use local plants and flowers in your garden. Why? They require less fertilizer and water because they've already adapted to your soil.

Spring into action. Keep your eyes peeled for discarded plants during spring clean-up time. Many people rip out their perfectly good plants to make way for a new garden design. Pick up these discards when you see them.

Ask for help. Your local landscapers not only know a tremendous amount about gardening, but they also know where they're tearing out plants that will go to waste—unless you ask for them. Say that you'll pick up the greenery and cart it away, and you may get some wonderful new plants for free.

Buy this summer for next spring.

Once the spring and early summer perennials have bloomed and faded at the garden store, look out for terrific bargains on plants that have shed all their blossoms. They can often be bought for as much as 75 percent off. You can plant them in late summer, let them get well established, and then you'll have a stunning array of new flowers come next spring.

Know what's growing before you buy. It's springtime and those nasty weeds in your yard are starting to sprout . . . only they may not just be useless weeds: they might be purslane, or, if you live in the Southeast, ramps (wild leeks), and they cost a fortune at the grocery store. Caveat: always make sure that what you're planning on cooking is, in fact, edible. If you're not sure, pull a few and take them to a local horticultural specialist.

Prescription medicine

Get a $4 prescription. Target, Walmart, and the pharmacies of many other stores across the United States have begun offering a list of more than 400 generic prescription drugs for $4 for a 30-day supply. The price of a 90-day supply is in the neighborhood of $10, depending on the pharmacy. You can get a list of the drugs available at the stores' websites or a printed copy at the stores' pharmacies. Ask your doctor if the drug he is prescribing is on the list—or if there's a suitable substitute on the list.

Buy at a wholesaler (even if you're not buying in bulk). Save money by filling your prescriptions at a wholesale club, even if you're not a member. The pharmacy may tack on a small fee, but you have the right under federal law to fill prescriptions at any pharmacy, so tell the person asking for your ID at the front door that you're only visiting the pharmacy. (But don't get carried away—you won't be able to buy anything else without a club membership ID.)

Do the splits. Ask your doctor if your tablets or pills can be split to save you money. You'll probably pay the same amount for the 10-milligram dose and 20-milligram dose, so if you buy the 20-milligram pills and split them in half, you've split your costs in half as well. (Note that you can't do this with time-release or long-acting pills or with capsules.) For best results, buy a pill-cutter at the drugstore, to make sure each pill is evenly divided.

Switch and save. Some pharmacies will reward you with discounts when you transfer your prescription from another drugstore. You may see advertised incentives to switch—like a gift card from your new drugstore.

Be loyal. You can score substantial savings if you're a repeat customer at a particular pharmacy. One major retailer we know offers discounts throughout the store for loyal pharmacy customers, and Kmart has tested a program that offers store-brand pain relief and cold medications for $1 if you purchase or refill a prescription at a Kmart pharmacy.

Ask for samples. Drug company representatives often shower doctors with samples of their medications, and your doctor is probably happy to share these free samples with you. Just ask if your doctor has any samples available. You'll save on a trip to the pharmacy, as well as on the prescription.

Go generic. You'll save big by using the generic version of your prescription drug. If a generic doesn't exist, ask you doctor if there is a similar, older drug that works just as well and is available as a generic.

Think like your insurance company. Request a copy of your insurance plan's formulary, or preferred drug list. You'll find drugs—both generic and brand name—that cost less and require a lower co-pay than drugs not on the list. Share the formulary with your doctor, and ask him to prescribe the drugs you need from the list, if possible.

Printer

Preview your savings. Don't automatically print a page from the Internet—it includes ads and icons you probably don't want. Instead, click on "print preview" or "print version" to see exactly what you're printing, then delete what you don't need. You'll save money on paper and ink as well as wear and tear on your printer.

Think about saving ink. Make your ink cartridge last longer by setting your printer to the lowest-quality setting possible.

Double up. To save paper when you use your printer, try printing on both sides. Or print on the blank side of already used paper. Better yet, don't print out at all: store e-mail messages and other potential printouts on your computer.

Produce

Weigh in on savings. Use the produce scale to weigh the packages of produce you plan to buy. That 5-pound bag of apples may not really weigh 5 pounds; it may weigh less (and if it does you shouldn't buy it) or it may weigh more (and if it does you should march it right over to the cash register). Always make sure you're getting (at least) what you're paying for.

Grow your own. There's no better way to save money and eat well than to grow some of your own produce. Instead of spending $10 a week on salad greens and vegetables and shelling out gas money to get to the grocery store, plant a few seeds in a small plot or in pots on your deck. You'll be mightily rewarded with fresh produce from April through November, depending on where you live.

Professional organizations

Join the crowd. Many professional associations offer discounts on health care, car rentals, and more to their members. Look at the type and quality of discount from the organizations for which you qualify to take advantage of these savings.

Quality

Always buy well if you can. It's true what they say: if you have a choice between buying something crafted well versus buying something shoddily produced, always opt for the better quality, if you can. It will last longer, won't have to be replaced, and likely won't have to be repaired as often as its cheaper sibling, thus saving you money in the long run.

Quantity

Two for one isn't always profitable. Before you grab "two for the price of one" in the grocery store, make sure that the individual price hasn't been elevated, too. And if you need only one (of anything), buy only one.

Radiator

Reflect on savings. Save on your heating bill by installing a heat reflector behind your radiator. (Create a reflector from foil-covered cardboard or by wrapping foam board in foil.) Make sure the foil faces away from the wall, and that the reflector is either the same size as the radiator or slightly larger. It will help push the warm air (that you've paid for) back out into your room.

Refrigerator and freezer

Vacuum up the savings. Be sure to vacuum the coils at the bottom or back of your refrigerator twice a year to keep the appliance working efficiently. You'll pay more if your refrigerator needs to work harder because of dust in the coils.

Extra fridge in the basement? Unless it's Thanksgiving or Christmas and you're entertaining a crowd, don't keep it cold "just in case." Pull the plug if it's empty, and sharply whittle away at your electric bill.

Keep it on the level. In addition to putting life-shortening strain on the mechanical parts, an out-of-level refrigerator can cause the doors to sag—or, if tilted forward, not close properly. Sagging doors don't seal properly, and expensive cold air will leak out, even if the gasket is fine. Place a carpenter's level on top of the fridge, and check it from side to side and from back to front. Inspect the legs or casters to be sure all are firmly on the floor. If one is not on the floor, or the refrigerator is not level, adjust the legs until the unit is level in all directions.

Keep the fridge clean.
Wash the compartments, drawers, and shelves of your refrigerator twice a year with a solution of baking soda and water. Also clean the drain pan with warm, soapy water. Wipe the door gaskets every couple of months. Be sure to clean up spills  promptly. Mold and mildew get harder to eradicate the longer they linger.

Keep a full freezer. It takes more energy to keep air at freezing temperatures than it does to keep solid items frozen, so you'll prolong the life of your freezer and reduce your energy bills if you keep the freezer packed. On the other hand, it's most efficient to leave room for air to circulate in the refrigerator compartment.

Give the condenser coils breathing room. Keep your fridge a few inches away from the wall so heat from the condenser coils will have plenty of room to vent away.

Test the door light switch. If the light inside your refrigerator doesn't shut off when you close the door, the heat of the bulb will keep the motor running overtime and will cause poor refrigeration. The switch has a button or a lever that's depressed by the door when it closes. You can check it by pushing it in by hand. Replace a faulty switch with a duplicate from the manufacturer or an appliance store.

Do a temperature check. To keep your fridge and freezer humming along at maximum efficiency, it's a good idea to take their temperature occasionally. Let a glass of water cool near the center of the refrigerator compartment for 24 hours. Then put a refrigerator-freezer thermometer in the water for a few minutes. Look for a reading between 34 and 40°F. In the freezer, insert the thermometer between two frozen food packages. Look for a reading between 0° and 4°F. If necessary, adjust the temperature setting and repeat the test.

Check the door gaskets. Your family probably opens and shuts the refrigerator dozens of times a day. All that use eventually causes the door gaskets—the rubber seals along the door's edge—to lose their resilience, letting cold air leak out. This makes the appliance work harder to cool more air, thereby shortening its life.

To see if the gaskets are doing their job, connect a 150-watt floodlight to a thin, flat extension cord. Turn the light on and place it in the refrigerator, pointed at one of the edges of the door, and with the extension cord leaving the refrigerator along the opposite edge. With the light on, the door shut, and the kitchen lights off, check for light seeping through the edge. Do this for each edge for both the freezer and main door. If any light is leaking out, the gasket is worn and should be replaced.

Generally, you'll need a gasket made for your specific model. Many appliance stores carry gaskets for the brands they offer, or can special order them for you. The replacement product should provide installation instructions. If an inspection of the gasket around your refrigerator door reveals just a small crack in a gasket that is otherwise serviceable, you can usually fill the crack with a little silicone caulk.

Rental cars

Take the shuttle to the car.
Renting a car at the airport—particularly in big cities—can be expensive. You can use the free airport shuttle to avoid this cost two ways: first, take the shuttle to your hotel and rent a car there. You can save about 10 percent on taxes and fees alone. Second, take the shuttle to your hotel, and rent a car the next day, thereby saving the cost of a full day's rental.

Time it right. When renting a car, try to fly in and out of the airport at the same time of day. That way you can avoid paying for an extra day of rental when you've used only a few hours.

Check your policy. You may not need liability coverage when you rent a car. Most insurance policies and some credit card companies offer liability coverage, so be sure to check your insurance and credit card policies before forking over money for what you may already have. Check for collision coverage, too.

Resorts

You pay to play. That resort on the beach looks so appealing, with unlimited golf, tennis, and swimming. But wait: you don't play golf—so don't choose a resort that features golf. The cost of golf will be built into the cost of your room. Choose a resort that offers the services and activities you'll use.

Go off-season. Get dramatically reduced rates and less crowded beaches and golf courses by visiting resorts in the off-season. Time your visit just before or after the high-rate season, and you can save big.

Rewards programs

Reward yourself. Join rewards programs whenever and wherever you can, whether offered by your credit card or an individual merchant or service you utilize often, to earn points every time you shop or travel. Then redeem your points for free merchandise, more travel, or services. Just be sure to note if the rewards program requires a membership fee, and determine if that fee is worth the rewards you earn.

Ribbons

Not just for the kitchen any more. Pull plastic wrap tight and twist it to make an unusual and inexpensive ribbon for your gift. It looks particularly festive atop a brightly colored package.

Do it again. High-quality fabric ribbons can be used year after year. Just gently iron them, and they'll look brand new.

All that glitters is . . . ribbon! Shop tag sales for cheap garments with sparkling or colorful fabric and cut them up with pinking shears for beautiful ribbons. You'll spend less on the tag-sale item than you will on new ribbon.

Rugs

Stay away from chemicals. Whether it's an inherited Persian rug from your great aunt or a fabulous flea-market find, steer clear of expensive industrial cleaners. If you find a troublesome stain, hold the rug up away from the floor, and pour warm water mixed with baking soda through the stain (be prepared to catch the liquid on the underside with a bowl). Rinse with clear water and blot dry with a clean, soft towel.

Shop early and save
12 clever ways to save money in the morning

Who knew that morning is the best time to save money? But it's true: All kinds of stores and service providers offer cheaper prices for their morning customers. And many household tasks save you money when done in the cool, fresh morning hours. Here's just a sampling of clever ways to save cash before lunchtime.

1. **Amuse yourself.** Many museums and botanical gardens, even theme parks and skating rinks, offer free or discounted admission before noon on certain days of the week, like Saturdays, when afternoon visits are proportionally greater than thinner morning crowds.

2. **Gas up.** You'll generally find the cheapest gas before noon. Big gas retailers set prices at about 10 a.m. or 11 a.m., according to Brad Proctor, the founder of GasPriceWatch.com. Proctor says gas prices go up right before noon about 93 percent of the time. In addition, buying gas in the morning, when it's cooler outside, gets you slightly more fuel, because the gas has more density than when it is warmer. And with gas prices as they are, every little bit helps!

3. **Grab some chow.** While you're gassing up, you might actually want to treat yourself to breakfast on the go—many gas stations offer "loss leader" deals on coffee and an egg sandwich or bagel and cream cheese for a dollar—less than you could make the same meal at home. With gas prices as high as they are, stores want to build customer loyalty, and offering

cheap eats in the a.m. is one way to do this.

4. **See a movie.** Some large theater chains offer discounts on tickets for movies that screen before noon.

5. **Fire up the oven.** Avoid creating unnecessary heat and humidity in the house during summer days by doing oven and stove-top cooking in the cooler morning hours—then reheat your dish in an efficient microwave, which won't heat up the house. You'll save on cooling bills by not making that air conditioner work harder. Ditto for doing the laundry and running the dishwasher.

6. **Give the garden a drink.** Giving your rhododendrons and roses an early-morning watering saves money on water because the liquid is more readily absorbed into the ground in the a.m. hours. It will evaporate more quickly in the noonday sun, which could mean watering again later in the day. Plus, any residual water left on the leaves by a morning watering will quickly dry out, preventing fungal and bacterial issues that can arise from evening watering—saving money on fungicides and other garden chemicals.

7. **Get your 'do done.** Some hair salons and barbershops offer early-bird specials to customers willing to come in for a clip before 11 a.m.

8. **Go shopping.** Many stores have their "loss leader" sales in the early morning hours. You've seen the circulars: "Wool cardigans, $12, 7 a.m.– 10 a.m. only." Some even reserve their drastic clearance sales for morning hours— "take an additional 75% off clearance racks between 8 a.m. and noon." Of course, this is only worthwhile if you need what's on sale! If you are food shopping, you might save some money by doing it in the morning before you get really hungry. Afternoon shoppers, ravenous for dinner, have a tendency to buy more food they don't need!

9. **Hit the gym.** Early-morning hours at the gym are very busy—everyone wants to get a workout in before the workday begins. From nine or ten until noon, however, many gyms are ghost towns. Sign up with a gym that offers discounted membership fees for those who pump iron during "off-peak" hours—you'll slim down, but your wallet will fatten up!

10. **Make doctor appointments.** The cost of the visit will not be cheaper per se, but you won't have to wait as long if you get there first. And time is money—you're out the door sooner and have more time to spend doing something else!

11. **Find your inner artist.** Local art and craft schools offer "morning bargain" classes that are less costly than afternoon or evening enrollment costs.

12. **Get baked.** Visit your local bakery as soon as it opens and see what goods from the previous day are selling for half or even two-thirds off. These items are perfectly fresh and wholesome—and they can be frozen to extend their shelf life.

Salt

Use kosher salt and save. Inexpensive kosher salt is not only tastier than regular table salt, but it's also more frugal. Why? Each flake or crystal of kosher salt is far bigger than its table-salt cousin, meaning that a single pinch will go a very long way, saving you dough in the long run. (One box lasted one of our interviewees over a year.)

Sandwiches

One is better than two. Share a sandwich with a friend when you're out and about and grabbing a quick lunch. One big sandwich costs less than two small sandwiches, so split the sandwich as well as the cost, and save!

Bring it from home. C'mon . . . bet your fridge is filled with assorted leftovers (ours is!). Why spend $5 for a mediocre sandwich from a deli when an inexpensive loaf of bread can be a vehicle for something you truly love?

Shades

Raise and lower to heat and cool. Save money on heating and cooling costs by using your shades and drapes strategically. In the summer, keep your shades and drapes closed on the sunny side of the house during the day and open at night. In the winter, keep them open during the day and closed at night.

Shampoo

Stretch your shampoo. You already know you should stock up on your favorite shampoo when it's on sale. What you may not know: you can alternate using your more expensive brand with a generic brand, and your hair will still look great.

Pump up the savings. Shampoo and conditioner bottles dispense more than you need. Pour these products into large pump bottles—they'll dole out smaller amounts so your hair care products will last longer.

Shipping

Add up the savings. Whether you're shopping by catalog or on the Internet, find a friend who wants merchandise from the same retailer and place a single order, then split the shipping fees. Better yet, find several friends and place a big order so you get free shipping.

Shoes

Join Project SOS: Save Our Shoes. Double or triple the life of your shoes by repairing them, resoling them, and reheeling them when necessary. Why buy a new pair of shoes when you can save your favorite old pair with new soles for $20 to $50? And don't forget that a shoe repair shop can fix luggage, belts, and purses, too.

Keep 'em clean. Watch WD-40 work double duty: it cleans shoe leather and lubricates it so your shoes last longer. Ditto purses, briefcases, wallets, belts, riding saddles, bicycle seats, leather car interiors, and leather furniture. You get the point!

Preventive shoe care. Place foam insoles into all your shoes to save their insides. Buy inexpensive store-brand insoles, and replace them when they become dirty or worn. You'll save money on new shoes, and you'll have more comfortable shoes as a perk.

Showers

Go with the (low) flow. Invest in a low-flow showerhead, and save on water and heating costs. By spending $10 to $20 on a new showerhead, you can save about 7,300 gallons of water and $30 to $100 each year on your water and heating bills.

Soap

Dispense some soap and some savings. Don't just refill your soap dispenser with soap. Add one part hand soap and three parts water for a soap that cleans without cleaning out your wallet.

Go the old-fashioned body wash route. Instead of using a separate bar soap for your body and one for your face, buy an old-fashioned liquid body wash, such as pure castile soap—a tried-and-true multipurpose favorite that's not only frugal, but also delightfully pure!

Socks

Getting dressed has never been so easy. Buy same-color socks in bulk. If the dryer eats one, you have an automatic match in your dresser drawer—and you won't need to buy a new pair of socks. Besides, you'll pay less buying packs of socks rather than individual pairs.

Soft drinks

Make your own. No, we're not kidding. Instead of buying chemical-packed flavored orange, grapefruit, or cherry soda, combine a splash of fresh juice with inexpensive club soda. Cheaper and healthier, by far.

Spices

Spice up your life for less. Never buy name-brand dried spices in the grocery store: you're paying for the bottles they're packed in. You can often buy spices in bulk at natural foods stores or ethnic groceries, or visit online spice suppliers such as kalustyans.com or penzeys.com. Buy spices you use infrequently in smaller quantities. Store away from light in glass or metal containers.

Dry your own herbs for savings and flavor. Have a leftover bunch of parsley (or cilantro, rosemary, or basil) in your fridge? Don't throw it away: dry it. Put the leaves on a clean baking sheet and place in a very low oven (200°F) for 30 minutes. Remove, crumble, and store in an airtight jar, out of direct sunlight.

Sponges

Microwave your sponge. Make sure your sponge contains no metal fibers, and, if it doesn't, put your wet sponge in the microwave for one to two minutes on full power. You'll kill the bacteria that would normally make you toss the sponge. You'll use each sponge longer.

Sporting goods

Make an exchange.
Look for school
and community
organizations that offer
sporting goods swaps.
You can also find sports
stores that sell perfectly
good secondhand
athletic equipment, such
as skis, for great prices.

Stockings

Freeze your hose. Panty hose, that is. Fill a plastic bag
with water, drop in your new stockings, zip up the top,
and toss the bag in the freezer overnight. Thaw the
concoction at room temperature. You'll strengthen
the fibers in the stockings, cut down on runs, and save
the cost of additional pairs of hose. You can continue
protecting your stockings by refreezing them once a
month, without water, for one night.

Stocking stuffers

Make Santa work all year. Buy stocking stuffers that
aren't overtly seasonal at half-off after Christmas, and
you can use them as small Valentine's gifts, in Easter
baskets, or as party favors throughout the year.

Storage

Store it well and save. Whether it's food, sweaters, or
garden tools, it pays to keep what you own stored
carefully to avoid spoilage, moth damage, or rust.
Double- and triple-wrap cold food items before freezing
to prevent freezer burn; store sweaters in sealed plastic

How long should your appliances last?

Check out the average life span (in years) of your:

Refrigerator/freezer
- Side-by-side: 14
- Top-mount: 14
- Bottom-mount: 17
- Single-door: 19
- Compact (dorm type): 5

Range
- Electric: 17
- Gas: 19

Dishwasher: 10

containers to prevent visitations from winged creatures; wipe down your garden tools with rubbing alcohol, dry them, and hang them until next year.

Stove

Stay small. Use small pots on small burners to save money on gas or electric costs. If you use a 6-inch pan on an 8-inch burner, you'll waste more than 40 percent of the energy. If you need to use a bigger pot, be sure to use a bigger burner; the pot won't heat evenly if you use it on a smaller one.

Cook on top. Your stove uses less energy than your oven, so try cooking meals on the stove as much as possible. Better yet, use a toaster oven, microwave, slow cooker, or pressure cooker.

Use elbow grease, not abrasives. If a spill has had a chance to dry out and cook for a while, use a sponge along with a solution of dishwashing liquid and warm water or a 50-50 solution of vinegar and warm water. An all-purpose cleaner such as Fantastik is fine to use, but don't give in to the temptation to grab that can of abrasive powder—you'll scratch the surface. The next spill will grip the scratches and be even harder to remove.

Look for a blue flame. If the gas flame on your stovetop burners is blue, they are working at top efficiency. If the flame is yellow, the burners are working inefficiently, and they should be adjusted by a service technician.

Prevent boilovers.
When cooking, use pots and pans that are deep enough to prevent boilovers and splattering. Minimizing spillage will minimize cleanup work and help prolong the life of your stove.

Clean spills quickly. Get in the habit of wiping down your stovetop after every use—your stove will gleam like new for decades, and you'll save yourself plenty of scrubbing.

Fix enamel chips. If the enamel on your stove gets chipped, touch it up with a porcelain enamel repair kit that you can buy at your appliance store. Be smart, and do it before the damaged spot becomes rusty.

Scrape with plastic. When food splatters on the heating element of your gas oven, grab the plastic ice scraper from your car to scrape it off. A metal scraper is likely to damage the element.

Clean that grimy oven window. A dirty oven window reduces the efficiency of your stove because you keep opening the door to check the food. To clean the window, rub it with a damp cloth dipped in baking

continued on page 158

The essentials of a successful tag sale

"All this clutter! All this unused stuff! I've had it!" Sound familiar? Last we checked, somewhere between 99 and 100 percent of American adults threaten to have a garage sale at some point in their lives. Ahh, but so few actually do it! Which is too bad, because having a garage sale can be loads of fun, deeply satisfying, and surprisingly profitable. Particularly if you follow our expert secrets.

GET THINGS READY TO SELL

If you've been to a tag sale where the sellers just plopped things out to sell without any preparation, you've undoubtedly been repelled by grimy appliances, dirty toys, and greasy glasses. Use the same standards for your sale items that you'd want a store to employ.

As you pull things out for sale, check them to see if they need cleaning or minor repairs. It is easier to do this as you collect things, rather than tackling it all just before the sale. Polishing metals, cleaning glass, removing stains, ironing linens—all will result in higher sales.

Hang 'em high. Clothing should be mended, cleaned, and ironed, and especially should be free of odors. Hang clothing properly, with buttons or zippers fastened, collars neat, and shoulders square on the hangers. Sweaters or items that might "hang" out of shape should be folded neatly and displayed on a table. Clearly mark the size of each piece, and hang or display according to size, gender, and age.

Run a load. Run plastic baby or toddler toys through the dishwasher. No one wants to buy a sticky, dirty toy for their child. Ditto for all dishes, glassware, tools, utensils, pots and pans, and storage pieces. Carefully wipe down and shine all gadgets and kitchen electronics.

Clean off the outdoors. Hose off outdoor furniture, garden tools, pots, and so on. If the cushions on your patio furniture are faded, at least be sure they are clean.

PRICE IT RIGHT

Don't wait until the day before the sale to price things—this will add to your stress, and you're more likely to over- or underprice something if you are doing a lot in a hurry. As you gather and clean things, think about the price.

Make it clear. Either purchase colored adhesive dots or use masking tape; the first is faster but more costly. If you're using the colored dots, you can either write the price on each dot or come up with a price for each color, and hang posters around your sale explaining the system. Use a permanent marker for writing prices—it's easier to read.

Tag it! Every single item, no matter how small, needs a price tag. If you have a lot of similar small items you plan to price equally, you can group them in a bowl, box, or basket. Be sure to post a small sign giving the price.

Sell the set. Price sets of things, such as drinking glasses, flatware, or dishes, so that it's to the customer's advantage to buy the set (Glasses: 50 cents each or six for $2). Group things that relate to each other, such as a bread maker with serving baskets and a butter dish, and sell

Items with a big draw

A few items traditionally seem to be in demand at tag sales. Here are some examples:

ANTIQUES. Check prices online or visit antique stores. Clean antiques cautiously—the patina of age can raise an object's value; overcleaning can devalue it.

COLLECTIBLES. Again, research to maximize your selling potential. (One easy method is to see what prices your items fetch on eBay.com.) Baseball cards, old toys or boxed games, coins, old vinyl records or album covers, comic books, out-of-print books, tools, and dolls can all be worth more than you think.

CHILDREN'S STUFF. Fashion dolls and baby dolls, doll clothes and furniture, stuffed animals, horse statues, children's furniture, tea sets, dress-up clothing, books, and art supplies generally sell well.

GROUPS OF THINGS. Some things—bottles, buttons, and salt-and-pepper shakers, for example—can sell faster than individual items. Try grouping closely related items, such as a group of old medicine bottles (especially if the labels are intact) or a group of metal military buttons.

SEASONAL DECOR. Holiday decorations, particularly for Christmas, are eternally popular.

ELECTRONICS. Television sets, VCRs, DVD players, CD players, personal stereos, microwave ovens, toasters and toaster ovens, surge protectors—clean them and be sure they work and they will usually sell. Used computers are much less salable.

FURNITURE. If clean and unbroken, furniture often moves fast. Clean all upholstery and plump cushions, polish wood, and wipe plastic or vinyl furniture. Desks, bookcases, chairs, side tables, dining tables, patio furniture, chests of drawers—fix them up, and you'll clear them out.

them as a set—the perceived value is higher, so you can charge a bit more.

Price them right. So how much should you ask for things? The standard rate is anything from 10 percent to 50 percent of what the item would cost new. It all depends on the condition of the piece and how much it is in demand. Since you want to sell your stuff, be careful not to overprice it, but also don't give it away, especially at the beginning of a sale. You can always lower the price toward the end of the sale day. But raising a price mid-sale is a definite no-no.

Deal or no deal. Decide ahead of time if you're willing to haggle. Generally, folks that frequent tag sales are ready to bargain, so you should try to be flexible. As you sort your items, make notes about things you're willing to reduce and things you are not willing to reduce. A well-placed sign at your sale saying "Make Me an Offer" may help you move your things faster.

ADVERTISE, ADVERTISE, ADVERTISE!

A tag sale is neither fun nor useful if no one comes to it. You have to go all out and create a crowd to get rid of your stuff and make real money. The trick: Get onto the "go-to" lists of all those regular garage-sale shoppers. Here's how.

Newspapers. There is a section of the classifieds devoted to yard, garage, and tag sales—and serious shoppers clip them out and go to the sales.

Online. Input "tag sale" (or garage, yard, or rummage sale) and the name of your town and state, and you'll be amazed how many sites pop up. Choose popular sites, like Craigslist. org, and advertise your sale.

Flyers or small posters. Check local ordinances about putting up posters advertising your sale. If you're given the go-ahead, cover the notices with clear contact paper to keep them looking good regardless of the weather. Put posters on school or church/synagogue bulletin boards (ask the office

DISPLAY TO ADVANTAGE

As the big day approaches, you need to plan how to display your merchandise. If at all possible, set up tables ahead of time so that, on the morning of the sale, you can simply move them out to wherever the sale will take place. If this isn't possible, sketch a map of the area you'll be using, and plan ahead where each piece will go—this will speed up everything on the day of the sale and will prevent you from forgetting things or displaying them poorly in the flurry of the last moment.

Display tables. You will need lots of table space to display your wares. Card tables, folding banquet tables, picnic tables, Ping-Pong, or other game tables—whatever you have can be made to work. If you don't have tables, make temporary tables by putting flat sheets of plywood or flat doors on top of sawhorses.

Set the stage. Arrange the tables so that people can browse between or around them easily. Bookshelves also work well to display all sorts of items.

first), community boards at stores, laundromats or dry cleaners, and local restaurants. Use bright, fluorescent-colored poster board, and make sure each sign gives complete, easy-to-follow directions to your house. A simple map can help. And finally, a day or two before the sale, put a big, double-sided sign on the most well-traveled street nearest to your house noting the sale, the times, and the address.

Color it up. Inexpensive, brightly colored plastic tablecloths, stapled or taped smoothly over the top surface, are a quick way to make your sale items "pop."

Look down. Don't forget the space below the tables when arranging your things. Baskets, large pots, stacks of puzzles or games, luggage, tins, and so on can all be arranged attractively underneath the tables, leaving the tops free for breakable, more valuable, or smaller items. Do not pile things in boxes or other containers— this makes it too hard for a customer to see what you have.

Like to like. As you plan your display, use common sense and logic and what you know of stores to help you figure out the order. One area could be a "Kid Zone" where you display clothes, furniture, toys, games, and so on, all related to children.

High couture. To display clothing, use a clothesline, a dowel between two taller bookcases, or a clothes rack so you can hang the clothes at the right height. Special pieces, such as a wool coat or prom dress, should be hung face out to show them off; other things can be hung as in a closet, separated by gender and size (and season, if appropriate). Again, you can create "sets" to add value: a jacket, scarf, and mittens or a fancy dress with a shawl and clutch purse.

Safe and sound. Valuable or highly breakable items, such as crystal, expensive jewelry, and antiques should be set close to the checkout table and out of the strolling aisles. That way you can keep an eye on them, both to protect them and to prevent

them from "walking away." If you have documentation of an item's worth (a magazine article, original brochure, eBay listing of similar items), it can be helpful to either add them to the display or have them easily at hand to justify higher prices—and to demonstrate what a bargain the customer is getting.

Try and buy. If you're selling a small appliance or electronics, such as a radio, toaster, or hair dryer, be sure to place them on a table with a power strip, and run a heavy-duty extension cord to power up the strip, so customers can test items on the spot. If you still have the original box and/or the instructions, put them with the device.

THE BIG DAY

You've done all the preparations, cleaned and priced all your merchandise, advertised the sale, and arranged your displays. Now it's time to get selling!

Ready the site. If you couldn't do it ahead of time, move all the tables and merchandise into place.

Scout the route. Walk the site to be sure that the flow works, there are no tripping hazards, everything is clean and orderly, and nothing you don't want to sell is sitting near the displays.

Ample parking. If possible, park your car or cars in a neighbor's driveway to free up your space. Walk out into the street in front of your house and be sure the display looks attractive to passersby.

READY FOR THE CUSTOMERS

You don't want someone to leave the site because they are thirsty. Set out a cooler jug or bottles of water. If you have a big coffeemaker, set it up with coffee, sugar, and milk or creamer.

A nice atmosphere. Set up a boom box with some festive, but not intrusive, music (Dixieland, pop, chamber music, jazz piano).

Howdy, neighbor! Greet people with a smile and an invitation to take their time looking around. Be available but don't hover.

Dollar sense. Keep track of the money and the sales.

Assign a cashier. Use extra care when handling money. Someone should always be next to the cash box. Try to have a calculator or adding machine at the checkout table as well.

Supersale? If you have a big sale, have at least two people at the checkout table and others (with name tags or other way of identifying themselves) walking through the sale. If they will be allowed to sell things, consider having them wear cash aprons (canvas tool aprons from a home improvement store work well).

Gauge how the sale is going. If sales are slow and people mention high prices, consider reducing prices by a percentage. For at least the last hour, reduce all prices by 50 percent and let folks know you'll accept the best offer on anything.

continued from page 149

soda. If the stuff is really baked on, wipe the window with ammonia, let it stand for 30 minutes, then scrape it off with a plastic ice scraper. Don't use a metal tool.

Clean the stove parts regularly. Periodically give your stove parts an extensive cleaning. Wash the burner pans and other removable accessories (but not electric burner coils) either by hand in the sink or by running them with your next dishwasher load (if the owner's manual for your stove says they're dishwasher-safe). Carefully remove control knobs (usually by pulling straight out) and clean around the knobs' bases. Wash the knobs in hot, soapy water, rinse, and dry before replacing them.

Clean under the hood. If your stove doesn't have a sealed cooktop, food and grease will fall down under the burners. So remember to lift the cooktop (like lifting the hood of a car) to clean beneath it. Follow the owner's manual instructions for lifting the top without damaging it. Then clean the grease buildup with a sponge and warm, soapy water or a 50-50 solution of vinegar and warm water. Rinse with clean water and a sponge.

Replace burner pans with originals. When burner pans get grimy and stained, they don't reflect the heat upward (which decreases the efficiency of your stove). Shine them up by rubbing with a paste made from vinegar and cream of tartar. If the pans have become too stained to clean, replace them with original equipment, which you can buy at an appliance store.

Go easy on the oven door. If you slam it, you may spring the hinge or throw the thermostat out of whack. And don't rest that casserole on the open oven door—using the door as a shelf is another way to damage the hinge.

Extend the life of your continuous-clean oven. The key to keeping your continuous-clean oven looking great for many years is to be sure to clean up major oven spills promptly before they form a glaze that prevents the interior from burning off minor spills. When you have a major spill, follow these steps:

- Blot up as much of the spill as you can with paper towels. Do this while the oven is still warm and the spill is soft. Don't rub—any paper particles can clog the rough surface.

- When the oven is completely cool, spray it with an all-purpose cleaner. Work the cleaner in with a nylon-bristle brush or net pad, let stand for about 30 minutes, then scrub with the brush.

continued on page 164

Turn it off!

How to pull the plug on wasted electricity all around your house

You turn off the lights when you leave a room, unplug your appliances when you go on vacation, and run the dishwasher and the washing machine only when they're full. But your electricity bill is still sky high! What more can you possibly do to eliminate wasted electricity and bring those costs down? A surprising amount, it turns out! Start with these three golden rules:

1. FOCUS ON THE NUMBER "ONE."

How many clocks are there in your home? How many TVs? Computers? Refrigerators? Cell-phone chargers? The national averages are growing for each. For example, we now average more than three televisions per household, and today, that often means multiple cable boxes, DVD players, game units, and sound systems. If you are serious about cutting electricity costs, you need to simplify. Live with one refrigerator and one freezer. Share a laptop and a single printer. Use a wristwatch and unplug clocks. Be a one-television home. You'll not only cut bills substantially, but you'll also find life might get a little simpler and more enjoyable!

2. WATCH THOSE CONTINUOUSLY RUNNING AMENITIES.

Many homes today have aquariums that have at least three electrical attachments in constant use (lights, heater, and pump). Some homes also have water fountains, dehumidifiers in the summer and humidifiers in the winter, electrical fences for their outdoor pets, elaborate outdoor lights on timers, and more. Turn a few off—or merely use them less often—and you can save a surprisingly large amount of cash on your electricity bill. Review all the functions and machines you have been operating automatically, and second-guess your need for them to be on so much.

3. TAKE THE GLOW TEST.

Even when computers, microwaves, and many other appliances and electronics are turned off, they still have clocks, lights, and other functions that require electricity. So do this test: Take a nighttime, lights-off walk through your home, and count how many household machines are glowing. In the morning, do all you can to cut back on the glow. Turn the clock off on the microwave oven; power down your computer and its peripherals using a single power strip with an on-off button; unplug kitchen appliances you don't use daily. Shutting down and unplugging will save more in electricity than you might think!

Now turn your attention to the smaller—but equally important—no-cost ways to eliminate electrical waste and bring your electrical costs back down to Earth. Try these quick-and-easy money- and electricity-saving strategies for your washer and dryer, oven, air conditioner, lights, and more.

✔ In the laundry room

Wash cold. Wash the majority of your clothes in cold water instead of warm or hot. According to the Alliance to Save Energy, an energy efficiency organization, this easy change can save up to $63 per year for the average consumer. Air-dry clothes, if you can, for considerably more savings.

Lose the lint. If you must dry clothes in a dryer, always clean the lint filter after every load to maintain peak drying efficiency.

Separate heavy from light. Dry towels, bedspreads, and other heavy items separately from lighter-weight items to increase drying efficiency. A dryer will keep drying until the wettest, heaviest item is done. Sure is wasteful if one beach towel is keeping the dryer going when everything else in the load is dry and ready! Also, try drying loads of clothing made out of similar fabrics, since one type of fabric can take twice as long to dry as another.

✔ **In the kitchen**

Place your refrigerator strategically. Keep your refrigerator away from your stove or heating vents. Otherwise, the fridge will have to work hard to stay cold . . . and you'll pay extra money for that.

Microwave it. Microwaves use just 20 percent of the energy that conventional ovens require, and the likes of sweet potatoes and baked apples will taste every bit as good—as will all frozen foods.

Dispose of high bills. Run your food disposal with cold water. The cold water solidifies grease; the disposal then grinds it up and washes it down the pipes. You'll save money on plumbing bills, as well as on hot-water costs!

✔ **In the bathroom**

Test your showerhead. Time how long it takes to fill a gallon bucket. If it's less than 20 seconds, replace your showerhead with a low-flow model. This type of showerhead uses from 25 to 50 percent less hot water—and cuts down your water and heating costs.

Fix the drip. Is your faucet dripping warm or hot water? Fix it or get it fixed right away. Those little drops of water can add up—to 15 gallons of hot water a day. You're needlessly adding to your heating and water costs.

Turn the fan off. In the winter, a hard-working bathroom fan can suck the warm air out of the average house in just one hour, according to the Department of Energy. Turn off your bathroom fan—and your range hood fan, for that matter—as soon as it has finished its job.

✔ Lighting

Leave the lights on. You may already know that compact fluorescent lights (CFLs) use about 75 percent less energy than standard incandescent light bulbs and can last up to ten times longer. What you may not know: Turning off CFLs when exiting a room for less than 15 minutes costs more than leaving them on. So if you are likely to be back in that part of your house within a quarter hour, leave the lights on to save!

Use task lighting. Why pay to brightly light an entire room if you're working in just a portion of it? Instead, try focusing light only where you need it: on your desk when paying bills in your home office, under the kitchen cabinets when chopping ingredients for dinner, or on a side table when reading in bed.

Three is better than one. Put three-way bulbs into as many lamps as possible (assuming you're not using CFLs). This type of bulb helps you keep lighting levels lower when you really don't need bright light.

✔ Air conditioners

Clean or replace your filters. A dirty filter makes your air conditioner work harder while pumping out air that's less cool. Either buy a replaceable filter that you can remove and vacuum every 3 to 4 weeks or front the cash for new filters—at about $5 each, a small price to pay for electric bills that won't break the bank.

Don't pay to cool the basement. Shut floor heating vents in the summer if you use window or wall air conditioners. Otherwise, the cool air you're paying for will flow down through the ducts into the basement.

Keep the air dry for savings. An air conditioner removes humidity from the air, as well as cools your house. The less humidity in the air, the less your air conditioner has to work. Give your air conditioner a helping hand by not adding unnecessary moisture to the air—try not to bathe, wash clothes, or cook in the middle of the day, when your air conditioner is working its hardest.

continued from page 159

Don't lay foil on the racks. Don't try to keep your oven clean by laying aluminum foil on the bottom or on the racks. Air needs to circulate freely throughout the oven in order for food to cook efficiently. Also, the foil reflects heat, which can throw off the thermostat.

Burn the coils clean. Heating coils on an electric range usually don't need washing. Instead, turn them on high to burn off spills. If a spill is massive, wipe up as much as possible after the coil has cooled and then burn off the rest.

Give your microwave a drink. Put a glass of water (add a few slices of lemon for extra deodorizing power) in your microwave and heat it on high for about a minute, until the inside of the microwave is steamy. Let the water sit in the steamy microwave for about 20 minutes. This will loosen all the food particles and begin to dissolve stains. Wipe the inside of the microwave with a paper towel, and you're done.

Sweaters

Buy one when you need one. Sweaters generally show up in stores around July, along with other fall clothes. Why do you need a sweater in July? Wait until October or November when you need one, and you can get the sweater for up to 75 percent less. The same idea applies to bathing suits, which go on sale in March and get marked down in July.

No sweat. You know that baby powder can be an effective deodorant, but did you know that it can also protect white shirts from sweat stains? Simply sprinkle it on the underarm areas of the shirt, then briefly iron. The baby powder will stop dirt and oil from staining the shirt. (This works for the collar, too.)

Tasting party

Excite your taste buds and your wallet. Host an international tasting party to learn more about ethnic food and wine. Have guests bring dishes and drinks to sample. You'll expand your culinary horizons, have fun, and avoid the high costs of sampling food and drink at restaurants and bars.

Taxes

Go directly to the source. You probably know that you can get free tax help over the phone from the IRS (800-829-1040), but did you know you can get free tax help in person at IRS walk-in sites? You can visit irs.gov, click on "Contact IRS," then click on "Contact my Local IRS Office," and find an IRS Taxpayer Assistance Center near you.

Telephone

Go high-tech for (very) high savings. If you have DSL or a cable modem, download and install Skype software for free and call other Skype users all over the world from your computer—for free! You can also call the landlines and cell phones of non-Skype users at bargain rates. Visit skype.com for details.

Make saving a feature. How often do you use speed dialing? Has call forwarding come in handy? You probably don't need—or use—the many telephone add-ons that show up on your phone bill. Reevaluate each feature, drop several, and easily save $10 per month. Special offers from the phone company change all the time, so speak to a customer-service representative to evaluate your options.

Go all the way. If you have a smartphone, do you also need a landline? Cutting the cord on the landline will eliminate all the associated costs. If you get your phone service as part of a cable package, though, be careful. You might be getting the phone as a thrown-in bargain, and you won't be saving anything by getting rid of it.

Television

Simplify and save. Do you really need over 100 television channels? If you trade your current cable package for basic cable, you may save up to $500 a year.

A super deal for the Super Bowl. Wait until the weeks before the Super Bowl for the best deal on a big-screen TV.

Thermostat

Lower the temperature and lower your costs. The Alliance to Save Energy says that you can subtract about 5 percent from your heating bill for every degree you lower your thermostat during the winter.

Get with the program. You've heard that programmable thermostats can save you money—but how much? If you invest $70 in an Energy Star programmable thermostat, you'll save more than twice that in the first year alone.

Don't exaggerate. In the morning, turn the thermostat up to the temperature you desire—not a higher temperature in the hopes that your house will warm up more quickly. It won't, and your furnace will have to work harder to reach a temperature you don't even want (and that will cost you more).

Toilets

Test for leaks. Add a drop of food coloring to the toilet tank. Wait a few minutes, then check to see if the color has shown up in the toilet bowl. If it has, you have a leak—and it may be costing you up to 200 gallons of water a day. Save water and money by fixing the leak.

Take up space to save. If you have an older toilet, put a plastic bottle filled with water on the floor of the tank. Because the tank will require less water to fill, you'll save money on your water bill every time you flush. (Don't do this if you have a high-efficiency toilet.)

Tools

Priced for Dad, bought for you. Buy the tools you need when they go on sale around Father's Day in June.

Tag it. One of the best places to buy tools is at a tag sale. Keep your eyes peeled for everything from well-priced (but used) table saws and sanders to hammers with a history. Feel free to haggle.

Toothbrushes

No cavities—and a free toothbrush. Be sure to ask your dentist for a free toothbrush next time—and every time—you go in for a check-up. Most dentists are happy to give

The Reader's Digest Quintessential Guide

you one, and some will also hand out free toothpaste, mouthwash, and dental floss.

Traveler's checks

Use them when you don't travel. In your wallet, replace your emergency cash—that you may have used for impulse purchases—with a traveler's check. You're less likely to spend it than cash, which means you'll keep it for when you really need it (and not for something you really don't need).

Trees

Naturally cool your house . . . and your costs. Plant trees on the south, east, and west sides of your house, and save up to 25 percent on cooling costs. And here's an easy and inexpensive way to get trees: if you join the Arbor Day Foundation, you'll receive 10 free trees! Just visit arborday.org.

Underwear

Stock up during seasonal sales cycles. Just as retailers reliably put seasonal items on sale, they do the same with necessities like underwear. Since you're always going to need underwear, socks, and so on, stock up when you see a sale.

Upholstered furniture

Pull the shades. Protect your upholstered furniture—and your investment in that furniture—by keeping it out of the sun. The sun can weaken the fabric's fibers and colors, so arrange your furniture to limit its exposure to sunlight, or simply shut the shades.

Vacuum the floor . . . and the couch . . . and the chair. Keep your upholstered furniture clean to save money. Vacuum it weekly to get rid of dirt and dust, which can act like sandpaper, grating on the fabric whenever anyone uses the furniture.

Utilities

Get audited—and like it! Ask your utility company for a free energy audit. A representative will come to your house and explain what you need to do to make your home more energy efficient. You can save $100 per year by sealing leaks in windows and doors and insulating ducts—all of which your energy audit will highlight.

Ask for off-peak rates. Find out if your utility company offers cheaper rates for running appliances at certain hours—usually off-peak—and save.

Vacations

Make the switch. Trade your house with someone looking to vacation in your area, and you'll save on lodging, car rental (you can trade cars, too), and restaurant bills (you have an entire kitchen at your disposal!). Even if you pay up to $100 to list your house on a home-exchange website such as digsville.com, homeexchange.com, or intervacusa.com, you still come out far ahead. (And don't forget that you can view listings for free.)

Stick close to home. Vacation in your hometown or a nearby area. Have you seen all the museums near you? Hiked on all the trails in local parks? Visited nearby historical sites that you learned about in school? View your hometown with a tourist's eyes, and you can have a great vacation at a fraction of what you normally spend.

Ask for (free) help. Call or visit the website of the visitors' center or Chamber of Commerce in the area where you'll be vacationing. You can get maps, sightseeing brochures, and information about lodging, restaurants, and local attractions—even money-saving offers—for free. Call local information for the phone number or search online for the name of the area plus "visitors center" or "Chamber of Commerce."

Guide yourself to a great vacation. Bypass sightseeing tours that take you and your wallet for a ride. Instead, look for self-guided walking and driving tours at the visitors' center at your destination. You may find a free or inexpensive guided tour as well.

Vacuum cleaner

Bag it. Prolong the life of your vacuum cleaner by changing the bag when it feels about two-thirds full. Otherwise, the motor will have to work harder, since the air sucked into the vacuum passes through a bag filled with dirt.

Veterinarian

Two for one. Find out if your vet offers a discount for a multiple-pet visit. Bring your two cats in at once, but pay for less than two visits.

Vintage goods

Older is better. Call it what you want: vintage, antique, or simply used, you'll find amazing bargains on clothes, furniture, and other previously owned goods at thrift stores like the Salvation Army or on sites like eBay.com. Not only will you get a great price, but you'll also help the environment by buying items that might get tossed—and you won't be buying something that needs to be manufactured and transported. It's an all-around win!

Wall hangings

Look great and insulate. Think about energy savings next time you look for art for your walls. Using quilts or decorative rugs as wall hangings will help insulate interior walls and keep energy costs down.

Washing machine

Wash more to save more. Don't wash your clothes more often, just wash more clothes at once. You can save more than 3,400 gallons of water each year if you simply make sure your washing machine is full before you start it. If you need to wash a partial load, be sure to reduce the level of water accordingly.

Water

Bye-bye, bottled water. Save your money and the environment by passing by bottles of water in the grocery store. Instead, buy a reusable water bottle. Assuming a store-bought bottle of water costs $1, you'll recoup your costs after only eight or nine uses of the reusable bottle.

Pitch this idea. Keep a pitcher or bottle of water in the refrigerator so you'll always have cold water on hand. No more running the tap to get water that's cold enough to drink—and no more money down the drain!

Turn off the tap. Turn off the water for two minutes while you brush your teeth or shave and save five gallons of water—and shave a few dollars off your water bill, too.

Weather stripping

Seal it for savings. Don't pay to heat or cool the air outside your house. Put weather stripping around doors and windows, and save about $30 per year in heating and cooling costs.

Wedding cake

Think small. Buy a small, exquisite wedding cake to cut in front of guests at the wedding reception, but serve a large sheet cake. The fancy and elaborate cake for the photos may be small, but the savings will be large.

Weeds

Shoot 'em dead. Make your driveway and sidewalks last longer by zapping weeds in cracks. Save money in the process by using vinegar in a spray bottle rather than expensive weed killers. (See also page 94 for another homemade solution for weeds.)

Windows

Sparkling clean and saving. Walk right by window cleaning fluid next time you visit the store. Instead, make it yourself: Mix ½ cup ammonia or white vinegar with 1 gallon of water. Then use crumpled newspaper with your homemade cleaner to wash and dry your windows. (See also page 90 for another homemade window cleaner.)

Wine

Make your case. Save 10 percent on your wine purchases by buying wine by the case. Many stores will give you 15 percent off if you pay with cash. And don't think you have to buy 12 bottles of the same wine. At nearly every wine store, you can mix different kinds and still receive the discount.

Wineglasses

Split entertaining costs. Do you have a neighbor or friend who likes to entertain but would like to save a few dollars doing so? Ask if she'll buy matching wineglasses with you. You each buy 12 and lend them to each other as the need arises.

Your wardrobe

BUYING CLOTHES

11 strategies for finding flattering garments at a reasonable price

1. **Buy next year's attire now.**
    To save loads of money on your clothing purchases, go shopping toward the end of the selling season. For instance, buy your spring and summer duds in July or August rather than in March, when prices are highest. This will mean some planning and forethought—you're going to get most of the wear out of these new clothes next summer. But the payoff is enormous.

    So when exactly are the selling seasons for clothing? Michael Laimo, formerly of Mercury Beach-Maid, a New York City sportswear wholesaler, says that there are two major selling seasons that apply both to men's and women's clothing:

- Spring/summer: March through the end of August.

- Fall/winter: August through February.

However, women's clothing also has "transitional seasons," which are influenced by weather:

- Summer into fall: August through October (dark clothing with short sleeves).

- Winter into spring: March through April (long sleeves and bright colors).

2. **Invest in one great garment.**
    From those slick magazine ads, you might get the idea that you have to spend a mortgage payment on a single outfit if you want to look stylish. Not so, says Los Angeles clothing designer Bobette Stott. Here's the key to controlling your clothing costs: Buy one key piece of high-quality clothing that you will dry clean and fuss over.

This garment should last you for years. For a man this item could be a jacket, a good sweater, or a sport coat. For a woman, it could be a great blouse, a jacket, or a nice cardigan sweater. Mix and match your high-quality garment with inexpensive, washable clothing that you replace every couple of seasons. With this approach, you will be investing only in one exquisite, showcase piece of clothing, but it will lend its class and style to anything else you wear.

3. **Avoid "one size fits all" clothing.** The idea of "one size fits all" clothing sure sounds attractive: You can't go wrong, right? Buy it, and you know it will fit!

Actually, most manufacturers who label their clothing this way are pulling the wool over your eyes. You will usually find this designation on lower-priced clothing, mostly on tops for teenagers. Here's what manufacturers are up to: It's easier—and therefore cheaper—to mass-produce and inventory a garment when it's all in one size. But the only garments that are truly "one size fits all" are some socks, which are made of fabric that's stretchy enough to adapt to a broad range of foot sizes. Otherwise, when you see "one size fits all" on a garment, keep shopping. Look for higher-quality clothing that will last a long time.

4. **Buy online to get deep designer discounts.** The clothing market is swamped

with garments that vendors need to unload. This is good news for you, because it means you can buy almost any designer clothing online at a big discount. When you shop at a brick-and-mortar retailer, you are footing the bill for the store's rent, employees' salaries, cushy carpet, and fancy display racks. Online vendors are no-nonsense, product-shipping businesses that do not have all of the overhead and decorative trimmings.

So here's how to get exactly the designer clothing that you want at a fraction of the price: Go to your local department store or boutique. Try on the duds that you like and write down the designer's name, a description of the garment, and the size. Then go home, fire up the computer, and conduct an online search for the designer. If the garment you are looking for has been in the stores for just two or three months, you should be able to buy it online for 50 to 75 percent off the retail price.

5. Use these strategies and your clothes will always be on sale. Many of us are programmed to take store pricing at face value. If you see a pair of trousers on the rack priced at $48, well, that's what it's going to cost you to take them home, right? No. The truth is that clothing stores are so desperate to move their merchandise these days that you can take home just about any garment at a discount—if you know how to go about it. Here's how to take advantage of a clothing store's flexible policies:

• Take a full-priced garment to the checkout counter and ask them to hold it for you until it goes on sale. Many stores will accommodate you, and you will be assured that they won't sell out of your size.

• Go ahead and buy the item you want at full price, but keep the receipt in an envelope in your car. Two weeks later, drop into the store with your receipt in hand. If your garment has gone on sale in the meantime, go to the register and ask for credit.

- Make friends with one of the salespeople at your favorite clothing store. This clerk will be able to alert you to upcoming sales, and will keep an eye out for the kind of clothing you like. Selling clothing has become difficult enough that he or she will work like the dickens to get you to buy merchandise.

- If you're making a big purchase at a department store, go ahead and get the extra discount they offer for accepting a store credit card. The card will qualify you for future discounts, too. But be sure to pay the balance off immediately so you don't have to pay finance charges; store credit cards often have exorbitant interest rates.

6. **Buy classic jeans.** When you buy a pair of jeans, put on a pair of blinders so you won't be distracted by all of those trendy styles that involve fading, weird cuts, peculiar colors, and even intentional rips. Manufacturers love it when you fork over cash for this trendy clothing because such jeans go out of style in a heartbeat—and then you have to buy a new pair in whatever the new style is. Instead, buy classic five-pocket, blue-denim jeans. These will last you for years, and even when they do fade, you won't mind, because they will look totally natural.

7. **Check the nap.** Your suit looks funny, but you just can't put your finger on why. Not all manufacturers pay attention to the direction of the nap of fabric—the way the fibers lie— particularly garment makers in developing countries. When you're buying a suit, says Ingrid Johnson, a professor of textiles at the Fashion Institute of Technology in New York City, here's an easy

way to test whether the fabric was cut running the same way in both pieces: Run your hand across the fabric in the suit jacket and then in the same direction across the skirt or pants. For instance, you might stroke from top to bottom on a sleeve of the suit jacket and then top to bottom on the skirt. The fabric may feel rough, or it may feel smooth—either is okay. But you want to be sure it feels consistent on each piece of the suit. If it doesn't, find another suit.

8. **Color-test duds before buying.** When you buy a garment in a store, conduct two quick checks to make sure the coloring in the fabric is high quality: Slip on a pair of sunglasses (the brown-tinted variety work best) to make sure the colors in the clothing still match. Then walk the garment over to a window and check that the colors match in daylight too.

Why bother? Though shoppers rarely hear about it, manufacturers spend a lot of time fretting over a quality issue called *metamerism*, says Johnson. You see, good manufacturers and retailers make sure that colors of a garment match in all light sources. Here's the problem: A garment may be made of a few different materials all in the same color—say, a jacket exterior, the cuffs, and the piping. Those different pieces need to all match, whether the light source is incandescent, fluorescent, or natural light. If you buy a garment and it doesn't pass this test, you have a right to return it.

Be especially careful when you buy clothing in an off-price outlet. That "bargain" garment could be marked down because it has a serious color problem.

What clothing retailers don't want you to know about pricing

You know the shopper's mantra, "Never pay retail," right? In case you've ever doubted this bit of wisdom, here's an inside glimpse of how retail pricing works for clothing.

It's impossible to know precisely what a particular retailer paid for the garments on display, but the pricing process works like this: Say a shirt comes in with a suggested retail price of $60, preprinted on the hang tag. Early in the selling season, the retailer will put that shirt on display for that price. Out of all of the people who end up buying that shirt, only 10 to 20 percent of the buyers will pay this original price.

Once you factor in sales and coupons, the price of the shirt starts creeping lower and lower. By the end of the selling season, that shirt is marked down to about $20, which is about what the retailer paid for it. But don't feel bad for the retailer—the store's bean counters have their eye on the average selling price of the shirt through its entire sales cycle. The retailer is happy if that average hits twice the wholesale price.

So the next time you consider buying clothing that's not on sale, ask yourself: Is it worth waiting a month or two (and risking my size selling out) if I can get this garment at a 60 or 70 percent discount?

9. **Slip into something old.**
Open up the yellow pages and jot down the addresses of vintage clothing stores in your area. If you care about the way you dress, it pays to prowl such stores regularly, says Birgit Muller, an Emmy Award–winning television costume designer. First of all, clothing from the 1950s and 1960s is usually better quality than modern garments. Such classic clothing keeps coming back into style, too, so it's a good investment. You'll be guaranteed a unique outfit—there's zero chance that you'll run into someone else at a party wearing the same dress. Also, vintage clothing is a particular boon for petite people, since clothing was sized much smaller then than it is today.

10. Shop to hide your bulge.
Want to disguise that "spare tire" building up around your midsection? These wardrobe tricks will help:

- Don't wear corduroy, velvet, or any other material with a nap (raised fibers). This adds bulk to your shape and makes you look wider.

- Avoid satin or any other shiny material, which will accentuate bulges.

- No plaids.

- Wear loose, dark fabrics that hang well—preferably silk or high-quality rayon.

11. Buy wrinkle-free, satin-weave cotton. Nobody wants to go to work in a dress shirt that looks like you've slept in it. Textile expert Ingrid Johnson says that there's actually a special kind of cotton that resists wrinkles—but chances are that a store clerk will have no idea how to identify such a garment for you. Satin-weave cotton, which is more common in women's clothing than men's, feels smooth under your fingertips. But to be sure you're getting satin weave, here's a quick and simple test, says Johnson: Grab a handful of the cotton fabric, squeeze, then let go. Does the fabric hold those wrinkles? If so, that's conventional cotton.

Does the fabric spring back relatively wrinkle-free? If so, you've found satin-weave cotton.

CLEANING CLOTHES

6 ways to keep your garments looking good longer

1. **Don't clean your clothes out of habit.** Many people believe that you should wash a garment every time you wear it. But that's a waste of effort and detergent. When you get home from work, change into your T-shirt and jeans, then evaluate your work duds before you toss them into the hamper. If your clothing passes this five-point check, you can put it on a hanger, air it out for two hours, then return it to your closet:

- Does it need repair? Any rips, missing buttons, falling hems, or broken zippers?

- Does it need a dry cleaner's care? Tough stains, particularly oily ones, should be taken to the dry cleaner within a day. If you wait weeks, your odds of getting the stain out are reduced dramatically.

- Does it need to be laundered? If the garment shows any of the routine smudges and dirt that come out in the wash, drop it into the hamper.

- Does it pass the sniff test? Yes, steel yourself and sniff the armpit of that shirt.

- Does your body need to be washed? If the answer is yes, then chances are the clothes that were hanging on that body need to be washed too.

2. **Lighten up on laundering and soap.** Detergent companies don't want you to know this, but most of us are chronically overwashing our clothing. We're wasting time and money (and detergent!),

and we're wearing out our clothes faster. In reality, most clothing only needs a touch of spiffing up. Do your regular wash using half the package-recommended amount of detergent, and set the washing machine at the lightest setting. When you have clothes that are truly filthy, use the full measure of detergent and a longer setting.

3. **Ease up on the laundry extras.** Household product manufacturers try to sell us all kinds of special washing aids, but clothes don't really need those dryer sheets and that fabric softener. The fabled "static cling" is not as horrible as the TV commercials will have you believe. If you do encounter garments that cling to each other because of static electricity, just dampen your hands and brush them across the material to kill the electrical charge. Towels will absorb water better if they are not doused in fabric softener; cleaning cloths work better without softener, too.

4. **Determine how clean your dry cleaner's facility really is.** If your clothes come back from the dry cleaner with a funky odor, your first move should be to take off the plastic covering and hang them up in the open— preferably outside on the back porch. There are two possible reasons for this odor:

- The cleaner didn't dry all of the solvent out of your clothes. Not a big deal. It will evaporate now.

- The impurities weren't filtered out of the dry-cleaning solvent, and you have dirt from someone else's clothes stinking up your garments. Yuck!

So let your clothes hang in the open for two hours, then give them the sniff test. If they're still stinky after a couple of hours, your problem is with impurities, not solvent. Go to another dry cleaner. "Clothes should smell clean and fresh if the dry cleaner is running his plant correctly," Newbold says.

5. **Preserve your heirloom gown correctly.** The prom or your wedding is a warm memory, and now you want to preserve the gown you wore. Many dry cleaners will gladly charge you $150 to $500 for special protective packaging called "heirlooming." Typically, the gown is thoroughly cleaned and then sealed in plastic and arranged inside a nice, windowed box. But if this service is not done correctly, that precious gown could be ruined. Asking these two questions will help ensure that your gown will be properly protected:

- Do you perform this service yourself, or do you send it out? If your dry cleaner sends your gown out for servicing, that's actually a good sign. Some specialists in the business really know what they're doing. However, some dry cleaners buy heirlooming kits from suppliers so they can do the job on-site, and some of them may cut corners on preparing your gown.

Stain-removing tricks

You don't get to be an Emmy Award–winning costume designer without learning to think quickly on your feet. Birgit Muller has been nominated for six Emmys, winning three times for her work on *The Bold and the Beautiful*. Here are her in-a-pinch fixes for stained clothing:

- For an oil stain, sprinkle the spot with baby powder, let the powder absorb the oil, then brush the powder off.

- To clean up a dribble of solid food, makeup, or lipstick, wipe with a piece of velvet. Keep a handkerchief-size square of velvet in your purse for emergencies.

- Use a piece of white chalk to cover a stain on a white shirt.

- To remove an ink stain, spray the spot with hair spray, then launder.

- To remove a red wine stain, blot it with gin, then launder.

- To remove the odor of sweat from a shirt, mix 1 ounce (30 ml) vodka with 2 ounces (60 ml) water in a squirt bottle and spray it onto the armpits. "We used to use that trick on movie sites in the desert," Muller says.

- Will my gown be vacuum sealed? For long-term protection of the gown, all of the air must be removed from inside the packaging. Otherwise, the garment will turn yellow and deteriorate. If your dry cleaner is doing the work on-premises, ask whether he owns his own vacuum-packing equipment.

6. **Dry-clean your suits less frequently.** Your dry cleaner won't tell you this, but most people bring their suits in to be cleaned way too often. New York City fashion coach Susan Sommers often hears clients complain, "My suit looks like hell after only one season." When she asks how often they dry-clean their suits, the answer is inevitably, "Every two or three times I wear it." That cleaning schedule is just too frequent!

   If your suit is just a little wrinkled, use a steamer on it to relax the fabric—or have the dry cleaner press it for you. If you get a spot on your suit, try removing it with a disposable fabric-cleaning wipe before you take it to the dry cleaner. Try to dry-clean your suit only once per season.

STORING GARMENTS
5 guidelines for wrinkle-free clothes and orderly closets

1. **Strip off the plastic bags.** Never store your clothing in the plastic bags that come from your dry cleaner. Clothing needs to breathe, and the moisture that gets trapped inside that dry-cleaner bag can damage your garments. If you want protection for garments that you put in storage, go to a discount store and buy a breathable cotton garment bag.

2. **Get out-of-season clothes out of your way.** One problem with snatching up all of those department-store "bargains" is that your closet gets packed tighter than a tuna can. This is a problem, because your clothes need room to hang freely if you want them to

come out of the closet fresh and wrinkle-free.

There is one key maneuver for freeing up closet space: Find a place where you can hang spillover clothing from your closet. This

might be in an empty guest-room closet, a hall closet, or a hanging bar in the laundry room. Every spring and fall, rotate the out-of-season clothing out of your bedroom closet and into your remote closet. Then bring the newly in-season clothing into your bedroom closet.

If you are rotating your clothing out like this every six months and your clothes are still jam-packed in your everyday closet, rotate them into and out of remote storage four times a year instead of two. Keep only this season's clothing in your bedroom closet. Or keep only one month's worth of clothes in your closet. This means some clothing hanging in remote storage will actually be in season. That's okay—it will be put in rotation next month.

Be sure to review your everyday clothing needs. If you wear casual clothes five days a week, don't store your fine clothes (suits and sport coats, for instance) in your closet. Put them in the remote location with the out-of-season clothes.

3. Get rid of clothing you don't wear. As you are rotating your clothing, examine every item. If there's anything you haven't worn in a year—no matter how cute it is, no matter what fond memories it might evoke—get rid of it. You can't afford to have it cluttering up your home. Think hard about your lifestyle. If you are like most of us, you own much more clothing than any one human needs. Buy less and get rid of more. There's no need to open your wallet every time you encounter an incredible bargain.

4. **Know the right ways to keep moths at bay.** Unfortunately, the bug-repelling powers of cedar closets and chests are grossly overrated. Sure, a moth will run when it gets a strong whiff of cedar—but we bet you didn't know that that pungent cedar-y smell will peter out after a year or two. Reviving the scent requires sanding off the surface layer of the wood, and almost nobody bothers with that. "When

you can no longer smell the cedar, the moths can't either," says textiles professor Ingrid Johnson. By the same token, if a dry cleaner asks if you want to pay to mothproof garments that are going into storage, tell him, "No, thanks." Dry cleaners mothproof clothing by adding a liquid to the cleaning solvent they use, but the secret is that this treatment only lasts for a month or two.

The better way to store those wool and silk garments? Dry-clean them first, then slide them into mothproof garment bags, which are available for purchase from the dry cleaner, and at some discount stores.

5. **Before storing a garment, clean it.** Before you put a wedding dress or a prom dress into storage, dry-clean it. Even if the dress appears perfectly clean, you risk ruining the garment if it hasn't been dry-cleaned. You see, "invisible" stains—such as lemon-lime soda, white wine, even

sweat—will turn into yellow or brown spots over time. Such spots, once they develop, are just about impossible to remove. There's another reason for making sure that any clothing is absolutely clean before you stash it away: Moths and carpet beetles are not only attracted to natural fibers such as wool and cotton, but they also salivate when you offer them clothing that is soiled, stained, or sweaty.

X-rays

Examine your X-rays. Do you really need a complete set of X-rays every time (or every other time) you visit the dentist? Ask your dentist if you can skip a set of X-rays and save the cost.

Yardwork

Be a yardbird and save! Don't pay a pricey "landscape engineer" to do what will spend your calories while it saves your dough. Get out there and pull some weeds, plant some veggies, and care for your flowers. Most landscapers charge upward of $50 an hour; multiplied by an average of two hours and eight seasonal visits, you've just saved yourself $800!

Zippers

Zip up the savings. Don't automatically throw away a garment if the zipper stops working. Try surrounding it with Velcro; you'll avoid the work of ripping out the zipper and the cost of replacing the item.

Zipper pulls

Replace it with style. If the zipper on your jacket or your purse is missing the zipper pull, don't toss it. Simply replace the pull with a small key chain (or just the metal ring of the keychain), a metal ring sporting a charm, or easiest of all, a paper clip.

Zoos

Join the animals. Don't let the high price of zoos keep you away from the lions and tigers and bears. Find out if your zoo offers a day of free admission or pay-what-you-wish donation (like Wednesdays at the Bronx Zoo), corporate days (where employees of certain organizations get free admission on designated days), or memberships that offer admission year-round (plus other goodies) for the set price of membership.

Also Available from Reader's Digest

The most useful information in a most useful format, from the people who have been getting to the heart of the matter for almost 100 years.

The Reader's Digest Quintessential Guides—
The Best Advice, Straight to the Point!

ON SALE NOW

Expect the Unexpected—Know What to Do When You Need to Do It
- Prevent and handle accidents
- Cope with medical situations
- Quick repairs you can do yourself
- Stock the right supplies
- Keep your family safe

$14.99 • Concealed Spiral • 978-1-62145-248-5

AVAILABLE SOON

The Truth Behind the Foods We Eat and What to Choose for Optimum Health
- The enemies of good nutrition and the food heroes revealed
- Tips on shopping, storing, preparing, and serving
- Scientifically proven evidence of the link between good food, good health, and long life

$14.99 • Concealed Spiral • 978-1-62145-293-5

An A to Z of Lawns, Flowers, Shrubs, Fruits, and Vegetables
- What to grow where
- Design gardens for beauty and productivity
- Deal with plant diseases, pests, and weeds
- Pick the right tools
- And much more!

$14.99 • Concealed Spiral • 978-1-62145-291-1

Reader's
digest

For more information, visit us at RDTradePublishing.com.
E-book editions are also available.

Reader's Digest books can be purchased through retail and online bookstores.